G000054851

Getting into
Veterinary School

Getting into guides

Getting into

Veterinary
School

James Barton

9th edition

trotman | **t**

Getting into Veterinary School

This 9th edition published in 2013 by Trotman Publishing, an imprint of Crimson Publishing Limited, Westminster House, Kew Road, Richmond, Surrey TW9 2ND

© Trotman Publishing 2013

Author: James Barton

8th edn by James Barton published in 2011
7th edn by James Barton published in 2009
6th edn by Mario De Clemente published in 2007
5th edn by Mario De Clemente published in 2005
4th edn by James Burnett published in 2003
3rd edn by James Burnett published in 2001
1st and 2nd edns by John Handley published in 1999 as *Getting into Veterinary Science*

Editions 1–6 published by Trotman and Co. Ltd

British Library Cataloguing in Publication Data
A catalogue record for this book is available from the British Library.

ISBN 978 1 906041 92 2

All rights reserved. This book is sold subject to the condition that it shall not, by way of trade or otherwise, be lent, resold, hired out or otherwise circulated without the publisher's prior written consent in any form of binding or cover other than that in which it is published and without a similar condition including this condition being imposed on the subsequent purchaser. No part of this publication may be reproduced, stored in a retrieval system or transmitted in any form or by any means, electronic and mechanical, photocopying, recording or otherwise without prior permission of Crimson Publishing.

Typeset by IDSUK (DataConnection) Ltd
Printed and bound in the UK by Ashford Colour Press, Gosport, Hants

Contents

About the author

James Barton has been a Director of Studies and a careers adviser at Mander Portman Woodward's London college since September 2007. As well as being the author of MPW's *Getting into Physiotherapy Courses*, James has sat on interview and audition panels and given careers advice across a range of fields. This will be his fifth Trotman publication.

Acknowledgements

I would like to thank everybody who has contributed to the ninth edition of *Getting into Veterinary School*. I am particularly grateful to Lianne Carter and Petrouchka Stafford for their unwavering support, creativity, guidance and for their patience in listening to my animal idioms! I am equally thankful to James Burnett, Maya Waterstone and my family for their advice and practical support. I would also like to thank Natalie Wilkinson, Betsy Malamah-Thomas, Guy Beynon and everyone else who contributed to the previous editions of this book. Particular thanks should go to the staff and students at the UK veterinary schools, and to both UCAS and the RCVS.

James Barton

Introduction
'Do I have a cat in hell's chance?!'

Are you running around like a headless chicken? Champing at the bit? Or are you going about this like a bull in a china shop? Well, the aim of this book is to kill as many birds as possible with one stone. After all, there is truth in the idiom that the early bird catches the worm. The last thing you want is for your application to resemble a dog's dinner or even mutton dressed as lamb, and therefore one cannot overvalue the importance of meticulous planning. So if you feel like a fish out of water and have butterflies in your stomach about the UCAS process, don't despair: this guide is here to help you cope. And remember, stay positive – every dog does have its day. The last thing we want is for you to feel as though there's an elephant sitting on your chest! Be dogged in your determination and work like a beaver. If you horse around, feathers will fly. Focus on your own application. No one likes a snake in the grass! If you want to be the queen bee, don't be too selective with your choices – a bird in the hand is worth two in the bush.

All right, enough animal clichés for now, but it is important that you note that while the process of applying to veterinary schools will help to shape your future career choice, you should never let it get to the stage where it grinds you down. Aside from anything else, by the end of this book, you should have an answer to the feline question above and be the one who got the cream instead of using up one of your nine lives! And so to business.

About this book

Someone once said to me: 'If you are allergic to animals, being a vet might not be the best career path.' This might sound like a ridiculous statement, but it does make a half-decent point: make sure your career decision is well thought out. In 2011, there were 2,252 applicants for pre-clinical veterinary medicine entry at veterinary school. Of these, 971 were accepted, a success rate of 43%, and 146 were accepted through Clearing – however, these people most probably already held offers but narrowly missed the grades in the summer exams. For those aspiring to join the veterinary profession, the most important question is 'What can I do to make sure that I am in that 43% when I apply?' The aim of this book is to supply you with that information. However, there is no secret formula that will ensure success. The students who are accepted work hard to gain their places. They are motivated and determined, and their desire to work in the field of veterinary science is deep-rooted and genuine. Having said that, without adequate preparation, even the most promising candidate will not get a place if they do not fulfil the required criteria.

This book serves as a guide to help you with the complexities of a veterinary application. Like veterinary surgery, ample preparation is required, alongside an attention to detail, good knowledge, and with all the variables working together.

How to use this book

The competition for places on a veterinary science degree course is ferocious and the odds of getting in are not as favourable as on other courses. If you look at the University of Liverpool, for example, they received 1,550 applications for just **161** places in 2012. As you will see from Table 8 (page 118), applicant numbers are high. Therefore you are going to need to prepare thoroughly for this application, taking into consideration all aspects of the course in order to maximise your opportunity of studying veterinary medicine at university.

This book will discuss all aspects of the application, from how to research and prepare for your application, choosing your course and the application itself, to the interview, results day and information on fees and funding. In Chapter 8 there is advice and information for 'non-standard' applicants – mature students, graduates and retake students. We also look at potential careers within veterinary medicine, and, at the end of the book, there is a further information section and a glossary where you will find details of sources for veterinary medicine and definitions of any abbreviations relevant to your UCAS application for veterinary courses.

As with other books in this series, including *Getting into Medical School* and *Getting into Physiotherapy*, this book is designed as a guide to the application process as opposed to a guide to the profession. Your work experience is your opportunity to find out more about being a vet.

This book should in no way be seen as dissuasive. It is about getting into veterinary school – it is not designed to put you off and push you towards something else. The tone reflects a balanced mixture of realism and optimism. No one should underestimate the hard road that lies ahead. Getting into one of the seven veterinary schools in the UK (Nottingham became the seventh in 2006) is just the first stage on the route to becoming a qualified veterinary surgeon, with all the inevitable hard work and dedication that will follow in the next 40 years or so. The key to success lies within each individual.

Table 1 Student numbers 2012–13

		admissions		admissions (or later)		with a degree		on course		intercalated course		intercalated degree		graduating (2011)	
		Male	Female	Male	Female	Male	Female	Male	Female	Male	Female	Male	Female	Male	Female
Bristol	UK	25	88	0	1	3	10	119	403	2	13	8	36	19	84
	EU	3	3	0	1	0	1	5	13	0	0	0	0	0	1
	Other	1	1	0	0	0	0	1	11	0	0	0	0	0	1
Cambridge	UK	17	52	0	0	1	6	94	289	0	0	0	0	14	44
	EU	0	1	0	0	0	0	1	6	0	0	0	0	0	1
	Other	0	3	0	0	0	1	0	10	0	0	0	0	0	1
Edinburgh	UK	16	66	4	9	4	12	95	340	2	2	0	0	16	63
	EU	1	2	1	3	1	5	6	28	1	0	0	0	1	5
	Other	5	33	8	39	8	54	51	234	0	0	0	0	6	35
Glasgow	UK	21	67	0	0	0	2	118	247	0	2	0	6	24	42
	EU	0	1	0	0	0	0	1	4	0	0	0	0	1	0
	Other	16	42	0	0	7	37	53	173	0	2	0	0	7	30
Liverpool	UK	25	91	6	17	6	19	125	468	1	10	1	5	20	99
	EU	0	3	0	0	0	1	2	7	0	0	1	0	0	1
	Other	0	0	0	0	0	0	2	10	0	0	1	0	1	3
London (RVC)	UK	46	134	10	29	12	36	224	755	4	14	3	13	43	167
	EU	0	1	0	1	0	0	4	14	1	0	4	0	0	3
	Other	3	23	8	28	10	38	29	124	0	1	0	0	3	12
Nottingham	UK	25	69	0	0	3	7	117	336	0	2	0	0	16	65
	EU	1	1	0	0	0	01	4	8	0	0	0	0	2	3
	Other	1	11	0	0	0	1	5	42	0	0	0	0	0	0
Total		206	692	37	128	55	232	1,056	3,522	11	44	17	60	173	660

All data supplied to the Royal College of Veterinary Surgeons by the veterinary schools, as required by Section 5(5) of the Veterinary Surgeons Act 1966.

Academic ability is not merely a requirement; it is an absolute necessity. Unless you have the clear potential to study science in the sixth form, this book alone cannot help you. Students attracted to veterinary science should have a natural academic ability in the sciences. A confident prediction of high grades at A level is a great help, but even that will not be enough on its own to get into one of the veterinary schools. You will have to show proof of your interest, enthusiasm and commitment – you will have to show that this is what you really want.

So how do you know that this is the career for you and that you are not wasting your own and everyone else's time? If you are asking yourself this, your number one priority must be to become well enough informed about and acquainted with the work of a vet to ensure that you have made the right choice of career and to safeguard against regrets further down the line. And once you know this, what do you need to consider next?

- What are the factors involved in choosing a course? Have you considered all of them?
- What do the courses have in common?
- What are the factors that influence admissions tutors to come down in favour of one well-qualified candidate against another?
- What happens at interview?
- What about the various career choices open to the newly qualified vet?
- What do customers who use the services of a veterinary surgeon look for in a 'good' vet?
- Does this sound like the kind of profession that would suit you?

Putting academic skill to one side for a moment, would you feel comfortable dealing with your customers as well as with the animals? The first thing you learn in veterinary practice is that all animals bring an owner with them. How would you handle a sceptical Dalesman or an elderly lady who is anxious and watchful as you come into contact with her beloved pet? Animals play a crucial part in the lives of their owners and whether the vet handles this with tact and understanding will be the deciding factor in both their professional and their personal development. This book will help those who feel drawn to the career for sentimental reasons to understand the realities – good and bad – of being a vet and will enable you to evaluate whether you have what it takes to follow this path.

A feature of this book is real students' views. Many people who are now undergraduates on veterinary courses say that they would have appreciated knowing the views of people in their position when they were at school. Panels of students returning to their former schools to give careers advice often do not include a veterinary student. This book, therefore, includes several student profiles, the first of which is given below.

Case study

Paul is 21 years old and from Middlesbrough. He has just finished the second year of his veterinary course and is now moving on to the clinical years.

'There was nothing particularly outstanding about my application,' he recalls. 'I just had the right ingredients I guess. I had undertaken a lot of work experience and, having been to all the open days, I realised the importance of a variety of experience. There is a different challenge inherent in each. I didn't realise how much diplomacy was involved in being a vet until I met a farmer! What is crucial about these work experiences is they always seem to provide contacts. One experience leads to follow-up work and then it can feel like a rolling stone, which is perfect. What you need is a starting point. Be as flexible as you can be, as willing to work as the next person.

'My GCSE and A level grades were good and my BMAT [BioMedical Admissions Test] was strong enough to get an offer. I was lucky enough to get offers at both Bristol and the RVC [Royal Veterinary College], but as a northern boy I knew London was where I wanted to be next.

'I have loved the first two years of my course. They have been extremely hard work but the variety of what I have done has been unbelievable. I am extremely excited about the fourth and fifth years as I am getting closer to my goal. All those years focusing on work experience instead of a kick around in the park have paid off!'

1 | The bare necessities
What is the role of a vet?

This is perhaps the most pertinent question of all because the answer to that question reflects the considerable sacrifice in terms of time and effort that every vet makes. Every veterinary practice has to be organised so that someone is on call 24 hours a day, for 365 days a year. As one farmer commented: 'A vet needs to have a really good sense of humour to be called out at 3a.m. on a cold night to deal with a difficult calving and having to get down in six inches of muck!' It is certainly not a career for someone lacking in confidence, or who holds back and carries an air of uncertainty. Vets are still held in high esteem. The popular image of a vet is of someone working long hours, who is able and caring, whose charges are not too high, and who doesn't worry too much about bills being paid promptly! While this closing sentiment might be ambitious, the popular view is in fact the accurate view.

James Herriot (an English veterinary surgeon and writer) would probably do these words more justice at this stage: he reveals in his books what the profession really entails. In his first book, *If Only They Could Talk*, he reflects on the unpredictability of animals and indeed a vet's life as a whole: 'It's a long tale of little triumphs and disasters,' writes Herriot, 'and you've got to really like it to stick it . . . One thing, you never get bored.'

On another occasion, Herriot muses, with aching ribs and bruises all over his legs, that being a vet is, in fact, a strange way to earn a living.

> *'But then I might have been in an office with the windows tight shut against the petrol fumes and the traffic noise, the desk light shining on the columns of figures, my bowler hat hanging on the wall. Lazily I opened my eyes again and watched a cloud shadow riding over the face of the green hill across the valley. No, no . . . I wasn't complaining.'*

Some people grumble about the beguiling influence of the Herriot books. There is, however, a lot of cool reality in the pages laden with good humour and philosophy; so much so that one student described the effect of the books as leaving a 'cold afterglow'. Many professions would love to have a PR agent with the skills of Herriot writing on their behalf.

So what makes a good vet?

- Confidence
- Authority
- Composure
- Nerve
- Empathy – for both patient and client
- Versatility
- Focus
- Organisation
- Resilience
- Being well informed
- Knowing one's limitations
- Good judgement, i.e. prevention versus cure
- And, above all, a thick skin.

If you have these qualities, a career in veterinary medicine is a strong possibility. Vets are incredibly resilient people who deal with a variety of challenges on a weekly, often daily, basis. You must have confidence in your own abilities and your own judgement, but you must also have the strength to communicate effectively and authoritatively. Bear in mind that you will be calling the shots because you will be the expert.

A good vet can diagnose most things, but, if they cannot, it is their job to know who can. The secret is to know your own limitations. This is particularly important for the newly qualified veterinary surgeon. 'New vets,' according to experienced Cheshire farmer David Faulkner, 'must know when to seek help and be mature enough not to be too embarrassed, for there are always a lot of new things still to learn.'

The farmer's view

'Farmers know immediately if they are going to get on with you,' an experienced vet revealed. 'They look at the way you handle and approach the animals. If you can't catch them, the owner will lose confidence and you won't be allowed anywhere near the livestock.' A seasoned farmer confided: 'Give me a vet who doesn't wait to be asked and is out giving you a hand.' He added: 'If they are confident in what they are doing it soon comes across.' Farmers and animal owners generally like to have a vet who communicates well, has a sense of humour, is outgoing rather than shy and reserved, and is able to walk into any situation and have an answer. There is a stigma about women in the profession and the capability of female vets in large animal situations. The truth of the matter is that if you choose to specialise in this field (no pun intended), gender issues will disappear if you are confident and firm.

Prevention

Even with the technological advances of the 21st century, prevention makes sense. Animals simply cannot tell you when they are unwell, so a good vet will seek to promote preventive medicine whenever possible. Today there is a lot of knowledge about preventive health by diet and vaccination. Whole herds can be treated at the right time of year. Farmers expect their vet to look ahead and draw their attention to what will prevent disease: 'Look, October is approaching – why not vaccinate all the cattle and prevent pneumonia?' If you give this kind of advice you will inspire faith in those you are seeking to help. Additives can be administered in either feed or drink. This is much better than having to go through the trauma of injecting a whole farmyard of pigs! A vet can do a lot of good with vaccinations and treating deficiencies through the feed by replacing what is not there, improving not only productivity but also the welfare of the animals.

Most people will agree that prevention is better than cure, but sometimes this is a naive statement to make. Preventive medicine is costly, and farmers in particular have a reputation for being frugal. There is no doubt that preventive medicine is a good investment for the future, but in the aftermath of BSE (bovine spongiform encephalopathy), foot-and-mouth disease, and the collapse of much of their export market, farmers are anxious and, in many cases, unwilling to make the necessary outlay. Drug usage for cattle has fallen away. Often farmers do not approach the vet until there is an emergency and by then it might just be an exercise in damage limitation.

In today's busy world, with a general shortage of vets, it is not always easy to respond to this situation. It is said in the profession that you should try to take time to stop and let your eyes range over the flock or herd, looking for the one or two animals who do not fit into the general pattern and who seem out of sorts. There is also a lot to be said for encouraging good husbandry by advising on the housing of the animals. While the sign of a good vet is that he or she will have the latest drug information at their fingertips and knowledge of how to treat certain conditions, sound, informed and diplomatic advice will often earn the vet similar respect and kudos among their clients: 'Instead of me treating the animals' feet, why don't you improve that footpath?'

Small animals

Working with household animals can require a different approach. It is as much about counselling the owners as treating the patients, and, for that reason, interpersonal skills are a prerequisite. With pets, there is great variety: one moment you might be treating a reptile with a nutritional problem; the next, a cat losing weight might be brought in for tests and cause you to wonder if there might be a problem with its liver – or could it be cancer? A rabbit could be brought in – many are now regarded as house pets – and your initial diagnosis of myxomatosis might be confirmed. Or it could be something as mundane as placing a microchip in an animal for security purposes. Dental problems among the small-animal population occur quite frequently but obesity is also much more common than most people imagine. The vet has to advise and persuade the owner – however obstinate they might be – to reduce the animal's feed and bring it in for regular weigh-ins at the surgery.

A lot of animals are kept in busy urban environments, thus increasing the risk of pets being involved in road accidents. If a dog that has been hit by a vehicle is brought in, the 'crash kit' may have to be used. The doses of the most commonly used drugs are marked clearly on the crash box lid, the syringes are loaded, and everything is sterilised and ready. It is important to act quickly, but the true professional keeps calm; this is no time for the vet to fumble when decisive action can save the dog's life.

Arguably the most important quality required for this job is having a thick skin, especially in cases where an animal has to be euthanised. The ethical issues that affect our medical profession and the moral question of 'playing God' do not exist in the veterinary counterpart because it is often kinder to make these decisions for the good of the animal. You have to weigh up the animal's suffering against the owner's protestations and grief and your own conscience. A good vet must find that little bit extra inside themselves. It is crucial to deal with the owners in a compassionate yet effective way. It has often been said that the hope and trust of the owners are matched only by the trust and helplessness of the animals. Imagine dealing with a distraught child when he's told that his pet hamster must be put down. How do you show empathy amid the boy's flood of tears? How do you discuss it with him? Perhaps the boy's parents will let you attempt to explain how the hamster feels and that soon the small animal's pain will cease and the end itself will not be felt. Even when you know it is the kindest thing to do, giving a lethal injection is still one of the toughest parts of the job.

So why do you want to be a vet?

It's important to ask yourself this because if you become a vet you will be embarking on a career without riches or glamour. Perhaps for you it is about adapting and fitting into a way of life. Is this what keeps everyone focused during the long hours of study? An interest in and sympathy for animals is taken for granted by many commentators, but in reality it is the way you react to an emergency that puts your dedication to the test. It is all in a day's (or night's) work for a vet and there is no one to applaud you except the grateful, or perhaps less understanding, owner. In short, commitment is the key, particularly if – or perhaps that should be when – the going gets tough. As a vet you must feel that you want to help, cure and take care of animals to the best of your ability, whatever the weather and whatever the circumstances. It is the kind of commitment that will almost certainly have begun at a very early age and will have become stronger and more focused in your teenage and college years. Of course, while the vast majority of qualified vets are in general practice, this is not the only option open to you: you might equally choose to go into teaching, inspection or research. Yet no matter which option you pursue, the level of knowledge and commitment required is very high.

Case study

Alfie gained his A levels in 2010 and is now studying veterinary medicine at Edinburgh University. Alfie grew up in Surrey, in the countryside, and wanted to be a vet from an early age. With persistence, Alfie was able to get work experience in a small local veterinary surgery where, sadly, he had taken his dog Sam to be put down. This strengthened Alfie's resolve, though, and he wanted to help prevent other animals suffering with terminal illnesses. 'Seeing Sam die of stomach cancer was hard but it made me 100% sure that I wanted to help other animals not go through pain.'

Alfie changed school between his GCSEs and his AS level year and this helped him focus on the academic requirements necessary to get to university. He achieved four A grades and, after having two interviews at two different places, Alfie received an offer from both universities. 'What is important is that you are interested in your A level studies. If you are not then you will not get good grades. Equally, it might imply that a career in veterinary science is not for you.'

Alfie's work experience involved him doing whatever work he could do alongside the vet – anything from manual labour to shearing sheep. This gave him the opportunity to ask any number of questions to help him understand the veterinary profession from the point of view of the different people who come into contact with the profession.

Alfie has enjoyed the first year of his studies, but finds some of the work hard. 'The pace is different from A level, and it is not just a question of learning notes – they want to find out if we understand as well: not like school! Another thing that makes it harder is that my parents are not around to tell me to do my homework every night, and there are lots of opportunities to go out and enjoy life. Still, I think I am just about coping but I know that I'll have to work harder next term.'

2 | Horses for courses
Studying veterinary medicine

Given the competitive nature of entry into veterinary school, the idea that there is an element of choice may seem strange. Even when a candidate is fortunate enough to get two or three offers and has to express a preference, the eventual decision is often based on things such as family connections, the recommendation of the local vet or whether or not the candidate liked the school or its location on the open day.

Maybe decisions should be based on more objective data than this, but they seldom are. This might not be a bad thing, as decisions made this way often work out quite well. However, although the courses are not vastly different, it is surely sensible for the candidate to be aware of the typical course structure and what is involved. This could be useful at interview. Most importantly, a knowledge of some of the differences between courses could play a part in your decision should you get two or more offers.

All the courses leading to a degree in veterinary science have to comply with the requirements of the Royal College of Veterinary Surgeons (RCVS) for recognition under the Veterinary Surgeons Act 1966. This is necessary if the degree is to gain the holder admission to the register, which confers the legal right to practise veterinary surgery. It follows that the courses are fundamentally similar; most of the slight differences come towards the clinical end of the degree. This is quite a contrast to many other degrees where the differences can be much more marked.

Veterinary courses have a carefully structured and integrated programme with one stage leading logically to the next. This logic is not always apparent to the student, who may feel surprised at the amount of theoretical work in the early pre-clinical stage. Later, as you get into the para-clinical and clinical stages, it all begins to make sense. As one final year student commented: 'It's not until the fourth or fifth year that you suddenly realise "So that's why we did that!" '

The pre-clinical stage

The first two years are pre-clinical and include a lot of lectures, practicals and tutorials. The normal healthy animal is studied. A basic knowledge of the structure and function of the animal body is essential to an understanding of both health and disease. The scientific foundations are being laid with an integrated study of anatomy and physiology. This study of veterinary biological science is augmented by biochemistry, genetics and animal breeding, as well as some aspects of animal husbandry.

Veterinary anatomy

This deals with the structure of the bodies of animals. It includes: the anatomy of locomotion; cellular structure; the development of the body from egg to newborn animal; the study of body tissues such as muscle and bone; and the study of whole organs and systems such as the respiratory and digestive systems. Studying this subject involves anatomical examination of live animals with due emphasis on functional and clinical anatomy. Students spend a lot of their time examining the macroscopic and microscopic structures of the body and its tissue components. One student said: 'We seemed to look through microscopes for hours at various organs and tissues. At the time it was not easy to see the relevance, but later what we had been doing began to make a lot of sense.' There is not only detailed microscopic study of histological sections but also the study of electron micrographs of the cells that make up the different tissues.

Veterinary physiology and biochemistry

This examines how the organs of an animal's body work and their relationship to each other. This is an integral part of the first two years of the course. It is concerned with how the body's control systems work, e.g. temperature regulation, body fluids, and the nervous and cardiovascular systems. You can expect that your studies will include respiration, energy metabolism, renal and alimentary physiology, endocrinology and reproduction.

Animal husbandry

This extends throughout most courses and introduces the student to various farm livestock and related aspects of animal industries. The kind of performance expected from the different species and their respective reproductive capacities is investigated. Livestock nutrition and housing are studied, together with breeding and management. Students learn about the husbandry of domestic animals and some exotic species. Animal husbandry also involves animal handling techniques. These are important skills for the future veterinary surgeon since the patients will often be less co-operative than those met by their medical counterparts. They may even be much more aggressive than humans!

The para-clinical stage

This is sometimes referred to as the second stage. It follows on from the first two years in which normal, healthy animals are studied. Now it is time to undertake studies of disease, the various hereditary and environmental factors responsible, and its treatment. The third year usually sees the study of veterinary pathology introduced (although it sometimes begins in the second year) with parasitology and pharmacology.

Veterinary pathology

This is the scientific study of the causes and nature of various disease processes. This subject is concerned with understanding the structural and functional changes that occur in cells, tissues and organs when there is disease present.

Veterinary parasitology and microbiology

This deals with the multicellular organisms, small and large, that cause diseases, and with bacteria, fungi and viruses. All the basic aspects of parasites of veterinary importance are studied. Students also take courses in applied immunology (the body's natural defences).

Veterinary pharmacology

This is the study of the changes produced in animals by drugs (artificial defences against disease). It comprises several different disciplines including pharmacodynamics (the study of the mechanism of the action of drugs and how they affect the body), pharmacokinetics (absorption, distribution, metabolism and excretion of drugs) and therapeutics (the use of drugs in the prevention and treatment of disease). Some schools introduce this subject in the fourth year.

The clinical or final stage

The last two years of study build on the earlier years, with food hygiene being introduced while the study of pharmacology is deepened. The meaning of the phrase 'integrated course' now becomes apparent as all the disciplines come together. Medicine, surgery and the diseases of reproduction are taught by clinical specialists in the final stages of the course, and this part of the course is largely practical. More time is spent at the school's veterinary field station. In some cases you can expect to live at the field station in your final year. Much of the study will be in small groups.

You will be allowed to pursue particular interests; however, the main focus will be on the prevention, diagnosis and treatment, by medical or surgical means, of disease and injury in a wide range of species.

Some practical skills learned in the clinical stage

There are many important practical skills that students have to learn in the final clinical period. One of these is the ability to examine the contents of the abdomen through the wall of the rectum without harming or causing infection to the animal through carelessness. You might also learn to use an ultrasound probe to examine, for example, the ovaries. Another use of ultrasound is to listen to the blood flow and the foetal heart sounds in a pregnant sow. Ultrasound can also assist in carrying out an examination of a horse's fetlock.

Students, like the vets they hope to become, can be called out in the middle of the night to a difficult calving. If a cow cannot give birth naturally, the student can help with a Caesarean operation. Using a local anaesthetic allows the operation to take place with the cow standing, which makes the process easier to manage. Practical skill is also important with foaling. It is best if foaling takes place quickly because it is less stressful for the foal, and students are taught that all that is needed is a gentle but firm pull. Final-year students can assist with lambing, and even with the birth of twin lambs. There are many other examples, too numerous to mention.

General anaesthetic can be used for anything from the full range of horse treatments to vasectomising a ram. Many other techniques are also taught: for example, students might look at images of the nasal passages of a horse and see the nasal discharge from a guttural pouch infection. Another example is learning the right way to trim a cow's foot. All animals (that have them!) can suffer problems with their legs or feet. The experienced veterinary surgeon has to have the skill and confidence to be able to remove a cyst from a sheep's brain without causing a rupture.

No wonder, then, that at this final clinical stage students find that all the earlier preparation comes together and makes sense as clinical problem after problem requires you to think and reason from basic scientific principles. Examples such as these do convey the varied nature of the veterinary surgeon's work, but it is as well to remember that in addition to the physician side of the job there is a lot of routine 'dirty' work. Students have, for example, to help maintain cleanliness in the stables and enclosures of the field station. In due course, when you become a working vet, you may at some stage have to tramp round a muddy farmyard on a cold wet day carrying out blood tests on hundreds of cattle.

Remember that this summary of some of the clinical work encountered on the course is far from comprehensive and should not lead students to believe that this corresponds to a job description.

Extramural rotation (EMR)

This is sometimes called 'seeing practice' and the time is divided between farming work and experience in veterinary practice. Students are required during the first two years to complete 10 to 12 weeks of livestock husbandry, depending on which school they attend. Students usually arrange this experience themselves during their holidays, and on the whole they do not seem to have too much difficulty finding a place. Veterinary schools have lists of contacts in their own area with whom you can get in touch. A modest amount of pay can be arranged directly with the farmer.

During the third, fourth and final years of their course, students must complete approximately 26 weeks of seeing practice. This will be mainly with veterinary surgeons in mixed general practice, with much shorter periods in, for example, laboratory diagnostic procedures and one or two weeks in an abattoir. Casebooks have to be kept and presented at the final examination.

Notes on veterinary courses in the UK

Bristol

Students are based in Bristol for the first three years of the course, with at least one day per week spent at Langford, where students will be for the last two years. Some units in years one, two and three are taught by pre-clinical departments that are also responsible for teaching science, medical and dental students. This encourages cross-fertilisation of ideas and access to the latest research findings in other scientific fields.

Assessment: Mainly by examination, normally in January and June each year. Additionally, students are also assessed in DSE (directed self education) and in practical contributions such as the clinical rotations.

Resits: There is usually a chance to resit all or part of the examination in September if the required standard is not reached in June.

Intercalation: Students may interrupt their studies in year three or four to have a chance to intercalate in a science subject that they have studied in order to obtain an honours BSc.

Clinical training: The clinical part of the veterinary school is at Langford in the Mendip Hills, about 14 miles outside Bristol. The site hosts a wide range of small-animal, equine and farm facilities including first-opinion practices and referral hospitals. There is also a veterinary laboratories agency and abattoir on site. Students may be placed with leading local practices and farms during their lecture-free final year. The emphasis is very much on small-group clinical rotations. You will undertake 12 weeks of pre-clinical extramural practical experience with animals. These placements are undertaken on farms and other animal units, such as kennels and stables, during the holidays of years one and two. A further 26 weeks of clinical extramural studies (EMS) are undertaken during the holidays of the last three years of the programme. For the most part, the clinical study comprises placements in veterinary practice, but it also includes attendance at an abattoir and optional research placements.

Cambridge

This is the smallest of the veterinary schools. The course extends for six years and is divided equally between the pre-clinical and clinical parts. The first three years of the course cover the scientific basis of veterinary medicine. The initial two years are concerned with the basic medical and veterinary sciences, between which there is much common ground at this early stage, bringing you into contact with students from other disciplines. There are also more applied courses in farm-animal husbandry and preparing for the veterinary profession. For the third year, you can elect to study in depth a subject of your own choice from a wide range of options, leading to the award of the BA (Hons) degree at the end of year three. The flexibility of the tripos system is one of its most attractive features. The tripos system is a system in two parts whereby you need to complete both parts in order to achieve an honours degree at Cambridge.

Assessment: Examinations in the Easter and Summer terms depending on the year of study.

Resits: There is an opportunity to resit veterinary examinations in September.

Intercalation: An intercalated degree will be awarded to all veterinary students (not affiliate students). Approximately three years after being awarded, this will be upgraded to a master's degree.

Clinical training: The clinical training course is taught in the Department of Veterinary Medicine at the West Cambridge Campus on Madingley Road. The emphasis is on small-group practical teaching, often eight students in a group, in rotations. The fourth and fifth years' studies include microbiology, pathology, medicine and surgery. The final year is lecture-free with hands-on experience and a period of elective study and is continuously assessed. The farm-animal practice provides first-opinion clinical services to surrounding farms, including the university dairy farm just a few miles away. A farm-animal referral centre was opened in 2002. Advantage is also taken of the Queen's Veterinary School Hospital, a nearby Royal Society for the Prevention of Cruelty to Animals (RSPCA) clinic, specialist equine practices in and around Newmarket and the Animal Health Trust Centre. There are facilities for equine work and there is also a small-animal surgical suite.

Opportunities for research ensure that veterinary teaching is embedded in the latest, cutting-edge discoveries. At the end of the course, those graduating will receive membership to the RCVS.

Edinburgh

Established in 1823, the Royal (Dick) School of Veterinary Studies was the second veterinary school to be established in the UK and the first in Scotland. The 'Dick' school benefits from a collegial community alongside up-to-date techniques. As Edinburgh has American Veterinary Medical Association (AVMA) accreditation, the veterinary degree course (Bachelor of Veterinary Medicine and Surgery or BVM&S) gives undergraduate students the opportunity to apply their skills in different countries in the future, whether as a vet or in biomedical research, for example. Edinburgh is internationally recognised for its commitment to excellence through a strong base of research and teaching in a well-supported learning environment. The Easter Bush Campus incorporates a new, purpose-built £40million teaching building, small-animal, equine and farm-animal hospital facilities with both first-opinion and referral services, and the world-renowned Roslin Institute located in a new £60 million facility offering opportunities to carry out research supervised by pre-eminent researchers in numerous fields. In addition, Edinburgh has a unique comprehensive exotic and wildlife service.

Assessment: Professional examinations usually include a mix of written and practical components with contributions from in-course assessment, continuous assessment or project work.

Resits: There is an opportunity to resit degree examinations in August if the required standards are not met during the year.

Intercalation: Students with a special interest in animal disease can choose to interrupt their studies and complete a BSc (Hons) in Veterinary Science, usually after year two or three of the programme, which involves one year of advanced study in many different areas including: biochemistry, neuroscience, veterinary biomedical sciences or microbiology and infection. For exceptional students, there is the opportunity to study a one-year research MSc or an intercalated three-year PhD. Students can also enrol on one of the school's prestigious taught MSc programmes, which include Animal Welfare and Behaviour, Infectious Diseases, Conservation Medicine, Equine Science and One Health.

Clinical training: This begins at the start of the first year in the clinically integrated programme with training in examining normal animals across the common species, progressing to abnormal animals in later years. The lecture-free final year emphasises small-group practical, clinical experience where students undertake clinical rotations in the school's hospitals and support services, giving students practical experience in a wide range of disciplines. The final year is longer than the previous years and incorporates an externship and elective periods to allow focus on areas of individual interest. Students also produce a personal and professional development portfolio, which enhances their employability, encourages life-long learning and promotes professionalism.

Glasgow

Founded in 1862, this is one of the larger schools. It is located at Garscube, four miles to the north-west of Glasgow. The school is considered to be the top in Scotland and the top in the UK, so you will be taught by world-leading professionals. On the site are the pre-clinical and clinical departments, as well as the Weipers Centre for Equine Welfare and a small-animal hospital, and nearby is Cochno Farm and Research Centre, which is used by the university as an additional teaching facility. Some pre-clinical teaching is conducted at the main university campus near the city centre, which enables students to benefit from the opportunities at both sites. The faculty is one of only four veterinary schools in Europe to be accredited to British, European and American standards. In a National Student Survey in 2011, Glasgow students reported a 95% satisfaction rating.

Assessment: Examination by written and practical work.

Resits: These can take place in September of each year. A second failure may result in repeating a year; normally this is only possible for one year of the course.

Intercalation: At the end of year three, students may study for a one-year BSc (VetSc) honours degree before starting the clinical training. Eight subjects are available. A two-year intercalated BSc honours degree at the end of either year two or year three is another possibility.

Clinical training: The lecture-free final year maximises the opportunities for small-group clinical teaching around domestic animal cases. This takes place at the faculty's busy referral hospital and through EMS undertaken in practices and other veterinary institutions in the UK and overseas.

Special features: In the first two years students are expected to complete 12 weeks of EMS in the holidays. In the third, fourth and fifth year holiday periods, you are expected to complete 26 weeks of EMS.

Liverpool

This was the first veterinary school to be incorporated into a university structure and therefore the first to establish a university-certified veterinary degree. The Faculty of Veterinary Science celebrated its centenary in 2004. There are two degree courses leading to the Bachelor of Veterinary Science (BVSc) MRCVS: the D100, which is a five-year course; and the D101, which is a six-year course incorporating an intercalated BSc. Candidates are strongly advised not to apply to both on the same application. The options for intercalating include a BSc in Conservation Medicine and an MSc in Veterinary Infectious Disease and Control. These courses are also offered to students from other veterinary schools. In 2001, the faculty also introduced a three-year BSc (Hons) in Bioveterinary Science. Teaching on this course is shared between the Faculty of Veterinary Science and the School of Biological Sciences. Veterinary students spend the first three years of the course on campus in Liverpool studying pre-clinical and para-clinical subjects. The course is modularised. During the fourth and final years, the students are based at Leahurst, the teaching hospital on the Wirral Peninsula 18 miles away, which has facilities for equine and livestock cases and a small-animal hospital. First-opinion work (dealing with calls from clients) is undertaken at Fern Grove practice in Liverpool. There are two separate practices operating out of Leahurst, serving the large local equine population and the agricultural sector, and they also get referrals from all over northern England for horses with colic, skin tumours and orthopaedic conditions. Farm visits and investigations extend to the sheep farming areas of north Wales and the dairy farms of Cheshire and Lancashire. Leahurst is in close proximity to Chester Zoo and there is a strong interest in wildlife diseases and animal behaviour.

Assessment: Examination is both by examination and latterly practical.

Resits: Resit applications are encouraged. Resits are possible in September.

Intercalation: The veterinary sciences course can be taken with or without an intercalated year.

Clinical training: There is substantial practical work throughout the course. Twenty-six hours of EMS are completed between years three and five.

Study abroad: Students can currently apply to be part of the Erasmus programme and undertake three-month clinical rotations in years four or five. Opportunities currently exist with the University of Helsinki (Finland), École Nationale Vétérinaire d'Alfort (France) and Vetsuisse (a joint faculty between the Universities of Zurich and Bern, Switzerland).

London

The Royal Veterinary College (RVC), based in Camden Town and Hertford-shire, is the oldest (established in 1791) and largest of the seven UK veteri-nary schools and one of only two veterinary schools in England accredited by both European and US authorities. As one of the University of London's 19 self-governing colleges, the RVC is the UK's only independent veterinary school and it also has a Centre for Excellence in Teaching and Learning. The RVC has developed innovative approaches to learning, and students are equipped with the knowledge and skills needed to succeed throughout their working life. Students spend their first two years undertaking comprehensive pre-clinical studies at the Camden Campus, and then proceed to clinical studies at the Hawkshead Campus in Hertfordshire (north of London).

Assessment: The college uses a wide variety of assessment methods. Some of them are highly innovative and have been pioneered by the RVC. Emphasis is placed on practical work and students are tested by clinical examinations, oral examinations and spot tests as well as written examinations, including multiple choice questions (MCQs) and extended choice questions, problem-solving questions and essay questions.

Resits: A level resits are considered providing the student achieves the highest possible grade in the second sitting. Resits are also permitted during the course; students are required to pass overall to progress.

Intercalation: Students may intercalate a BSc after successful completion of, normally, the second year. Students can also be considered for certain BSc courses offered by University of London colleges or other universities, or for the RVC's own veterinary comparative pathology course.

Clinical training: In year three, students begin their clinical EMS at a variety of veterinary placements, eventually totalling 26 weeks (up to six of these weeks can be overseas) by the middle of year four. Lectures are timetabled early in the week. On Fridays students get the opportunity to get feedback on their knowledge using the computer-based MCQs. The tutorial system has been revamped recently and students take part in monthly groups of six to eight students. Most of the remaining time is spent gaining hands-on experience in RVC clinics and hospitals (intramural rotations). During year four, students also spend at least eight weeks devising and executing a research project on any aspect of veterinary science that interests them.

Nottingham

Based at the university's Sutton Bonington Campus, Nottingham's School of Veterinary Medicine and Science accepted its first students in 2006. It aims to equip students with all the necessary diagnostic, medical and surgical skills. In 2011, the veterinary school was ranked as the best for overall student satisfaction in the National Student Survey. Its course integrates clinical medicine and surgery with pathology and basic sciences, to ensure that its graduates gain the best possible foundations for a career in the veterinary profession. Studies include time spent at the new purpose-built clinical teaching facilities and with local clinical practitioners. The five-year degree course leads students from day one through a clinically integrated curriculum providing learning in all aspects of veterinary medicine and surgery. In years one and two, students undertake a minimum of 12 weeks' animal husbandry EMS and at least four weeks of clinical EMS in year two. All students undertake a research project in year three, and a minimum of 12 weeks of clinical EMS in both year three and year four. At the end of year three, students graduate with a Bachelor of Veterinary Medical Sciences (BVMedSci). The summer term of year four and the whole final year is spent in clinical rotations. This includes a minimum of 10 weeks' EMS. Another 25 weeks of intramural rotations are undertaken in year five, which is lecture-free. Intramural rotations may include time at both large- and small-animal practices, laboratory facilities and specialist facilities. After five years of successful study the degrees of Bachelor of Veterinary Medicine (BVetMed) and Bachelor of Veterinary Surgery (BVSc) are awarded.

Assessment: Using different types of assessment, Nottingham aims to measure a wide variety of skill and knowledge-based learning objectives. There are in-course module examinations including practical tests, essays and short projects. There are also informal assessment opportunities for students to evaluate their progress.

Resits: Applicants will be considered if they resit A levels. Resits during the course are available.

Intercalation: It can be possible to integrate a master's degree into the course.

Clinical training: Each student undergoes as standard 12 weeks of EMS in animal husbandry and 26 weeks overall of EMS in clinical environment.

3 | Separating the sheep from the goats
Preparation and experience

Wanting to become a veterinary surgeon is a long-term commitment. It requires perseverance and a lot of determination. If all goes well and you get the kind of sixth-form science results demanded by all the veterinary schools, it will still take a further five or six years to qualify. Most people faced with the need for intensive study in the sixth form will find it hard to look further ahead than the next test or practical. Yet much more than this is needed if you are to stand a chance of getting into veterinary school.

Starting early

Ideally, the pursuit of your interest in animals and their welfare – in short, your commitment – should have started much earlier than sixth form. There are numerous cases of aspiring vets who have begun their enquiries as early as the age of 12, and certainly many have started gaining their practical experience by the age of 14.

Some vets grew up on a farm and knew that they wanted this kind of life. Others come from an urban background and have developed an interest despite not being brought up in an animal-friendly environment. This interest can be kick-started in a variety of ways and can develop through, for instance, pet ownership, the Herriot books, one of the numerous television programmes such as *Animal Park*, *Super Vets* and *Vet Safari*, or the influence of a friend. 'It's a great life, there's so much variety,' was one student's view. 'You realise it when you start going out getting experience. You see that you can be a vet in a town or in the countryside, that some practices are much larger than others and that some are very busy while others appear more relaxed.'

One young vet said that she had begun her enquiries at about the age of 14 and started working at weekends – her experience began with work in a stables where she began to learn horse riding. Another recalled how she had done kennel work at weekends for four years before becoming a veterinary student. It goes without saying that cleaning out kennels is a dirty, often unpleasant job, but to do this over such a long period shows an impressive degree of commitment and dedication from an early age. Some students have the chance to gain early experience on a nearby farm. But what would you do there? One farmer's wife commented: 'We would expect a 14-year-old to help feed the livestock, to help with bedding-up, which means putting fresh straw in the pens, and sweeping up.' You should be alert to what is happening around you. Before long you may start asking questions: 'Why is that calf coughing? What are you giving it?'

Getting more experience

As those pre-A level years unfold, it makes sound sense to follow up your visits to the local stables, kennels or farm with a week or two spent with your local vet. The point is that you are not just trying to find ways to satisfy the admissions tutor at veterinary school who may one day read an application that you have completed, important though that is; you are also testing your own motivation. This is vital because, make no mistake, you are going to need all the focus you can muster. The task you are about to set yourself is going to draw upon all your commitment, dedication and determination.

It should be pointed out that students who are still at school or sixth-form college will be very lucky to find themselves in the consulting room with the vet. This is because anxious owners will not always appreciate or understand the need for someone of school age to be present. It is much more likely that you will be asked to spend time with the veterinary nurses. As one vet commented: 'Let's see if they can handle animals. Are they frightened?' The idea is to see how the student reacts to aspects of animal husbandry at an early stage. If you cannot abide cleaning up the blood and faeces that go with animal practice, then you should in all probability think of another career. After an artery has stopped pumping or diarrhoea has ended, there is a clean-up job to be done – this is an early experience for many well-intentioned potential vets. Can you take it?

Confirmation of a period spent at a veterinary establishment is one of the conditions for entry to an undergraduate course leading to the degree of Bachelor of Veterinary Medicine or Science. Without getting out and finding out what it is like to deal with sick animals as well as normal, healthy ones, how will you know that you are suited to a career dedicated to providing a service to animals and their owners? As one student put it: 'Knowing what animals look like doesn't necessarily prepare you for what they feel or smell like. There is only one way to find out and that is to get into close contact.' You may think you love animals because of the way you feel about your own pet, but going from the particular to the general may cause you to think quite differently. You might even be allergic to some animals. Make certain that you still feel happy about dealing with animals in general and that you really mean business.

Specific university requirements

Work experience is also vital if you are to have a chance of being called for interview, and without an interview you cannot be offered a place. Some of the veterinary schools are more specific than others about what they expect in the way of practical experience.

- The RVC specifies quality work experience over quantity. It requires two weeks of work experience in a veterinary practice and two weeks in a different animal environment (outside your home environment), such as a kennel, cattery, animal shelter, farm, stables, city farm, pet shop, lambing, wildlife park, zoo, etc. You do not have to have gained experience in all these areas. NB: This is a minimum requirement.
- Cambridge is more relaxed about work experience. The Cambridge website states that 'it is helpful to have some personal experience of the veterinary profession and have a realistic idea about what the work may entail. However, extensive experience is not a prerequisite and seeing a variety of different aspects of the profession for relatively short periods can be more helpful.'
- Bristol states that you must show evidence of work experience to justify an interest in the subject, although it is left up to the applicant to acquire as much practical experience as possible prior to interview. What they do require is for you to show that you have worked in a veterinary practice in addition to related work experience at a farm, stable, kennel, rescue or abattoir. You will then be tested at interview on your general knowledge gained from your work experience.
- Edinburgh expects applicants to have as much varied work experience as possible. This should be in both small- and large-animal veterinary practices; in livestock farms and dairy farms; in other places such as zoos, kennels, catteries, wildlife farms and stables; and a day at an abattoir is recommended but not expected. They go on to say that work experience in a veterinary or biomedical laboratory is also useful. It is not a requirement to complete a particular number of days, as this varies overall, and, while breadth is important, your work experience should not be to the detriment of your academic work.
- Glasgow advises applicants that 'experience working with veterinarians, so that the applicant has some understanding of the duties and responsibilities of a practitioner, is essential before making such a career choice'. They also say that they 'not only assess the breadth of candidates' experience of working with livestock and companion animals, but also examine personal attributes which demonstrate responsibility, self-motivation, a caring ethos and resilience'.
- Liverpool requires a minimum of six weeks of work experience relating to the husbandry of a range of animals, at least four weeks'

experience of veterinary practice, preferably spent in more than one practice, and a further six weeks of other animal experience, including farm work, in stables or kennels, etc. Zoo work and visiting abattoirs can be used as work experience but they are not essential. However, experience of UK farming practices is a prerequisite.

- Nottingham is fairly open-ended but requires at least six weeks of animal-related work experience. This could be in general practice, on a farm or at a stables, for example. They will consider references if sent.

Making the initial contact

Making the first contact can be quite difficult, often because of your nerves, inexperience or because the vet is cautious and reluctant to take on an unknown commitment. This is where parents can help, particularly when you are pre-sixth form. If a parent knows that their son or daughter is serious and is showing promise in the sciences at school, they can be a real help by speaking to the vet and giving reassurance. Generally vets will react favourably to a parent's call because it means that the contact is serious. Once the initial approach has been made, the next stage – developing contacts – is best left to you as part of your growing self-reliance.

Your local vet will know a lot of people through working with animals. A recommendation, or better still an introduction by your local vet to a large-animal practice or a local farmer, may lead to work in a stables or work with sheep, for example. You will get to know people yourself and this will build your confidence.

Developing contacts in this way is known as networking. Taking the initiative like this can do you more favours than always relying on the careers department at your school. However, it is worth checking to see whether your school careers department can help you. Frankly, some school careers departments are much better organised than others. If the careers programme is well organised and planned on an established contact basis, it would be sensible to enlist the department's help. However, do bear in mind that there is concern among some vets that placements organised by schools are not always carefully matched. If you have any doubts on this score, you will be well advised to take the initiative in making your own arrangements.

Remember that in the end it is your own responsibility to get practical experience. Busy people such as vets and farmers are likely to be more impressed with those who exhibit the confidence and self-reliance to make their own approaches.

What the vet will want

Some vets are reluctant to allow young, inexperienced people into their practice. This is understandable. They know that many people are attracted to the idea of becoming a vet; these people have, after all, seen many television programmes! Look at it from the vet's point of view. Some people are attracted to animals for emotional reasons; some may not be academically strong enough to make the grade; some may be so impractical that they could get their finger nipped through one of the animal cages in the first half hour. Do not be surprised if some vets suggest that you should first visit for just a day. The reason for this is that they feel they need to meet you first before committing themselves. As one vet said: 'You can get a fair idea in the first few hours; some are bright and a pleasure to have around.'

What will the local vet ask you to do? This will depend on the vet. 'We cannot afford to waste time so we begin by asking about their capability for science A levels at grades A*, A and B,' remarked one vet. 'We give them three days of blood and gore to see what it is all about. In our case, they will see a farm. We insist on wellies and a good standard of dress, no jeans or open-necked shirts!' Alternatively, your local vet may be a small practice dealing mainly with companion animals – most often cats and dogs, but also rabbits, goldfish, gerbils and budgies. Some students may themselves have gained experience breeding bantams, ferrets, pigeons or fish. This all points to a strong interest.

Some practices are mixed, dealing with farm animals, horses and pets, while in country areas there are practices that deal mainly with farm animals. The types of practice and their size vary widely. The average practice has three or four vets; however, at the one extreme about 2% have more than 10, each with a degree of specialisation, and at the other end of the scale, about 25% are single-handed practices, requiring practitioners to deal with a wide range of work. This being so, the resources that the vet will be able to draw upon will also vary widely.

Shaping up in the surgery

A head nurse in a medium-sized mixed practice uses the following list of questions to enable her or him to judge how students helping in the small-animal surgery are shaping up. They are all well worth considering to make sure you're fully prepared for work experience.

- How keen are they to help in every area? For example, do they clean up willingly?
- How observant are they? Do they watch how we do the bandaging or how we hold the animal straight ready for an injection? Do they watch carefully how we take a blood sample, administer an anaesthetic or set up an intravenous drip?

- Do they maintain a neat and tidy appearance and clean themselves before going in to see a small-animal client? This is very important to the owner.
- Are they friendly towards the client? Do they make conversation and try to establish a relationship?
- Do they ask questions about what they do not understand? They shouldn't be afraid to ask even while procedures are being carried out.
- Are they listening to what is being said and the way it is being said? Do they appreciate the experience that allows the vet to counsel owners on sensitive issues, for example on reducing their favourite pet's diet? This is not an easy message to get across to an overindulgent owner and a vet needs a good 'bedside manner' to be able to tell the owner what must be done without giving offence.

Checklist of experience

Always take up any opportunities that you are offered. Variety of experience will not only broaden your understanding of the profession you seek to join, but will also impress the admissions tutors when they come to scrutinise your UCAS application. Here are some suggestions. Remember, some applicants to veterinary school will have carried out a few of these suggestions four or five years before applying! Others are applicable only to Year 11 or sixth-form students. But if you can tick every box by the time you submit your form in October of your upper-sixth year, well done!

- Get work experience in catteries and/or boarding kennels.
- Work in the local pet shop.
- Make contact with a local vet and indicate your interest by helping with some of the menial tasks. If you are keen you will not mind doing the dirty work.
- Get at least two to three weeks' experience with a large-animal veterinary practice or occasional days or weekends over a long period. Without this, you will not be accepted into veterinary school, no matter how well qualified you are academically. You must also gain some experience of working in a companion animal practice. Some candidates are fortunate in having access to mixed practices in which they can gain familiarity with handling large and small animals.
- Visit a local dairy farm and get acquainted with farm work, which accounts for at least 30% of all veterinary science work. Try also to assist on a sheep farm at lambing time.
- Work with horses at a riding stables. (Remember that riding establishments are subject to inspection by an authorised veterinary surgeon.)
- Visit an abattoir if possible.

- Get in touch with one of the animal charities, such as the People's Dispensary for Sick Animals (PDSA) or the RSPCA, and find out about their work.
- Spend a day in a pharmaceutical laboratory concerned with the drugs used by vets as well as medics, or in a laboratory of the Department for Environment, Food and Rural Affairs (Defra).
- Try for any additional relevant experience that may be within your reach, e.g. at a zoo, where you could work as an assistant to a keeper, or in a safari or wildlife park.
- Make a point of visiting local racecourses and greyhound tracks, paying particular attention to how the animals are treated. Perhaps your local vet has a part-time appointment to treat the horses or dogs. If the offer comes to visit with the vet, you should take it.
- Visit country events such as point-to-point races, even if it is only to see what goes on. One day you may get an admissions interview and the more you know about what happens to animals in different situations the better.

Case study

Lianne studied at a sixth-form college in Sussex. Her love of animals started with King Charles spaniels, but as time went on this developed into a wish to learn about the palliative care of animals. She had a difficult time organising work experience because she was also teaching dance alongside her studies.

However, she prioritised and compartmentalised her time and sought out a variety of work experience. 'The hardest part of the work experience to me was working with large animals. As I am small it was a little daunting at first and I am sure this is not the part of veterinary medicine I wish to focus on. However, I am grateful for the experience as it toughened me up. I really enjoyed the time I spent in my local veterinary practice because of the diversity of the cases coming in. The ability to cope with a constantly changing routine is critical to becoming a good vet.

'I then went to work on a farm in North Yorkshire. It was through a friend's contact that I managed to get this but that is what it is all about, utilising contacts where you have them. What I found all of these experiences helped me to do was consolidate my thoughts on what I wanted to do. That is why selectors are so keen on it. The course is a massive undertaking and should not be embarked upon lightly.'

Variety and staying power

It is crucially important to demonstrate variety in your practical experience with animals. A visit of just one day to a veterinary practice where you watched small-animal work, followed by another visit to a mixed practice where you were able to see a surgical procedure carried out will be impressive, particularly if you can combine this with work at a stables, some contact with local farms, and at least some experience in, for instance, a kennels.

But your application to veterinary school will be enhanced even further if, in addition to this, you can demonstrate a convincing commitment to one or two of the local professionals. What will impress people is the fact that you have willingly returned to your local vet's practice over a period of time and only the vet will know what it has cost you to do this, and the admissions tutors of course. True, you will have seen a lot of interesting and varied activities and will have met many interesting people, but many of your friends would have melted away had they been asked and expected to do what you have had to do. Let's face it, not many students would have returned to the practice after having to clean up and deal with blood and muck time and again.

If you can demonstrate both a variety of experience and a committed staying power, there is no doubt that this will count strongly in your favour when the competition for places in veterinary school is at its fiercest.

4 | The 'Jack Russell' Group
Choosing your course

In order to gain a place at university, you must do your research into all aspects of the course. There is no substitute for preparation. There are only a small number of veterinary schools and therefore there is no excuse for a lack of reading into what the courses entail.

Choice of school

When considering which school to choose, you should look at the course, the teaching style, the applicant numbers and the entry requirements, and you should visit the university as well. Studying is an investment, both of time and money, so you must ensure that you can picture yourself at the school for the duration of the course.

Get hold of the prospectuses for these universities. These are free and universities are willing to send them to students. At the end of the day they are looking to attract the best students, so they will have marketing material. In addition to these prospectuses, there is also a lot of detailed information on university websites, so you might save yourself a job and find out about courses here. Keep in mind, however, that online information is constantly changing and therefore you might want to keep checking it until you submit your application, to make sure you are up to date about what requirements are expected of you.

Talking to admissions tutors is also an extremely useful exercise when choosing a university. They will be able to answer any specific questions you have, which will help you decide whether you have the best character fit to study there. But **do not** ask them for basic information that you could find out from the websites. That is a waste of their time and does not reflect well on you.

League tables for veterinary schools reveal only so much, as there are only seven universities offering the specific veterinary medicine course. However, they will tell you about the quality of research, facilities and student satisfaction ratings, important things to consider in the overall university picture.

Also, it is worth bearing in mind the campus and facilities when making your decision. Think of the distance from home, the distance from the city and the distance from amenities, and make your decision based on this as well. University is as much an experience as it is an academic institution. Try to picture yourself there!

Open days

You should visit the veterinary schools that hold special interest for you on their open days. Such a visit will give you the chance to see some of the work of the veterinary school. There will be special exhibits, possibly a video programme, and most probably the chance to hear the views of the admissions tutor. There may also be the opportunity to visit the veterinary school's own field station where most of the clinical work is done in the final stages of the course, and although veterinary students are kept very busy you may get the chance to speak to some of them. Some schools arrange for a number of their students to accompany parties of visitors on the open day. The open day will also give you an opportunity to see the general attractions of each university as a place to live and study over the next five (or six) years.

As with most things nowadays, everything you need to know is on the internet, so your first point of call must be the individual university websites to look for updated information on their open days. Your school will also receive details of open days with forms to be completed by those wishing to attend. If you have not heard by about a month ahead of the college open day you wish to attend, make enquiries in your school's careers department. If you hear nothing, you should take the initiative yourself and write to the school liaison office or directly to the institution that interests you. (See the contact information in Chapter 12.) You owe it to yourself to find out as much as you can. Your visit and how you felt about it could be a talking point should you be called for interview. So do not squander the opportunity to fit one or two visits into your A level study schedule.

If you are taking time out gaining practical experience and have already met the academic requirements, you may be able to attend more open days. If this is the case, you may find that you receive more than one unconditional offer and so you should certainly try to visit as many of these events as you can to help you make the best decision.

It is a good idea to make notes after each visit to an open day of your impressions and what differences you spotted. These notes will be very useful if you are called for interview – you will almost certainly be asked about your visit.

Course entry requirements

The academic requirements of the seven veterinary schools are similar, but there are some differences and it is important that you obtain the most up-to-date information before deciding where to apply. With regards to the course, be very careful that you are selecting the correct option as there are courses with pre-clinical years and Gateway pathways (see page 38) that will not necessarily be what you are wishing to study.

You can get information from:

- university prospectuses
- university websites (more likely to be up to date)
- *HEAP 2014: University Degree Course Offers* by Brian Heap (Trotman Publishing; publishing in May 2013)
- university admissions staff.

Typical student offers for the academic year 2012–13 are listed in Table 2 below.

For A level students, the selectors will take into account:

- GCSE grades
- AS choices and grades
- A level (A2) choices and predictions or grades
- documentation on any extenuating circumstances that might have affected your performance.

You will be asked for 'good grades at GCSE'. This means lots of A and A* grades, particularly in the sciences, English and mathematics. If you did not get good GCSE grades, you can still apply for veterinary medicine, but your referee should make it clear why you did not achieve the grades that you needed – there may have been circumstances, such as illness, that affected your performance.

Every university student has to meet the general matriculation requirements of each university (consult the prospectuses for details), but in addition there is the special prescribed subject requirement. You should check the requirements carefully – the veterinary schools' websites carry the most up-to-date information – but it is likely that you will need three A levels (that is, three subjects carried to A2 level), which will include Chemistry, Biology and one other science or mathematical subject. Your choice of AS and A level subjects is vital because, although one veterinary school might require three sciences (including Chemistry) at AS level with two taken on to A2 level, others will require Biology and Chemistry at A2, or even three sciences at A2. If you are applying to Cambridge, you should be aware that different colleges have different requirements.

Table 2 Typical student offers 2012–13

University	A levels required	A levels preferred	Preferred grades	Access course available	Subjects required	BTEC accepted	Widening participation policy
Bristol	2	3	A*AA–AAA+BMAT+AAB (Vet Sci+Pre Vet Yr)	No	Biology and Chemistry	Yes	Yes
Cambridge	3	3	A*AA+BMAT	No	Biology or Chemistry or Physics or Maths	N/A	Yes
Edinburgh	3	3	AAA	No	Chemistry (A) and Biology or either Physics or Maths	No	Yes
Glasgow	3	3	AAB	No	Chemistry (A) and Biology or either Physics or Maths	No	Yes
Liverpool	3.5	3.5	AAAb+AAAb (with Int Cal Yr)	No	Biology and other sciences	Yes	Yes
Nottingham	3	3	AAB+AAB (Vet Med + Prelim Yr)	Certificate in Health Sciences at Lincoln University	Chemistry and Biology and a third subject	N/A	Yes
London (RVC)	3	3	AAA–AAB+BMAT	Veterinary Gateway course	Chemistry and Biology and a third subject	Yes	Yes

Currently, no veterinary school makes a conditional offer on three A levels at below AAB grades. Unlike the requirements for many other courses, offers are likely to be made on the basis of A level grades only: stand-alone AS levels are unlikely to be taken into account. However, clearly the AS grades are important because they will be stated on the UCAS application, and thus will give the admissions tutors an indication that you are on course for AAA or higher at A level. For example, when faced with two candidates whose academic backgrounds are identical except that one has AAAA at AS level whereas the other has CCCC, who do you think they would favour?

The A* system

The A* system is a known quantity nowadays and universities increasingly use it as part of their requirements at undergraduate level, normally asking for A*AA. As you will see in Table 2, not all universities require an A*AA prediction but you should be aware that a lot of candidates will have this and so the grades that are published should be regarded as a guideline.

Some students have been known to query whether they should take a fifth AS level or a fourth A level (not including General Studies). Before taking another subject you should bear in mind that if you offer four A levels your performance in all four subjects will be taken into account.

So, if you do feel inclined to add a fourth subject at A level, remember the high grades needed for admission.

Other qualifications

For applicants with **Scottish qualifications**, it is likely that you will be asked for AAAAA in your Higher grades (SCE/SQA) and Advanced Higher grades in Biology and Chemistry. Some veterinary schools like candidates to take a new subject at Higher level if only two Advanced Higher grade subjects are taken in the sixth year. Higher grades alone are unlikely to be sufficient.

The **Irish Leaving Certificate** is accepted at certain universities. This is acceptable on its own or in combination with UK qualifications. You are expected to get AAAAAA and to include Biology and Chemistry.

The **International Baccalaureate** is usually acceptable, provided that appropriate combinations of subjects are studied. Three subjects are needed at the Higher level. They must include Chemistry and Biology, as well as ideally one or both of Physics and Mathematics. Grade scores needed at the Higher level are likely to be 7, 7 and 6. If the combination is likely to be different, advice should be sought. Similar subject combinations are required by those offering the **European Baccalaureate**. Applicants are likely to need a score of 80% to 88%, including Chemistry and Biology.

The **Advanced Diploma** in the following subjects will be considered at grade A alongside A levels in Biology and Chemistry (only at the RVC): business; administration and finance; construction and the built environment; creative and media; engineering; environmental and land-based studies; hair and beauty studies; hospitality; information technology; manufacturing and product design; and society, health and development.

Access to HE Diplomas must include at least 21 credits at Distinction and 18 credits at Merit and must include Biology and Chemistry. These must also be Distinctions in all modules taken.

> It is important to note that qualifications differ between all the universities and therefore you should visit the websites to find the most up-to-date requirements.

Veterinary Gateway pathway

The Veterinary Gateway pathway is a one-year course that is part of an extended six-year veterinary degree programme. It was specifically formulated for those students who are part of the UK Widening Participation cohort – a scheme to get more young people into higher education. It is not applicable to international students. The aim of this course is to get students who have not met the standard entry requirements and help them develop their skills over the course of an intensive one-year programme.

There is an eligibility criteria that you must meet. You must be from a non-selective state school, your parents must not have attended a higher education institution, and your total household income must be £25,000 or less. See www.rvc.ac.uk/undergraduate/vetgateway/index. cfm for more details.

5 | Take the bull by the horns in the cattle market
Applying to veterinary school

Admissions tutors try to get the best students they can for their course. That is putting it at its most basic. But there is more to it than that. They are also acting in the best interests of the veterinary profession. They know that the competition is fierce and that the biggest hurdle faced by aspiring students is entry into a veterinary school. Once this obstacle is overcome, there is, given the undoubted ability of those able enough to get the entry grades needed, every chance that with diligence and lots of hard work the student will in due course enter the profession.

However, it is important to understand that motivation is the key factor in selection. It is, in the last analysis, more important even than A levels or their equivalent. Therefore, admissions tutors look at the total impression conveyed by the candidate in their UCAS application. This will include not only academic predictions and their head teacher's report but also extracurricular interests as well as the extremely important supporting practical experience and references. Admissions tutors know that they are exercising a big responsibility: their decisions will largely shape the future profession.

Taking a broad view

Ideally, admissions tutors will seek to accept students representing a good cross-section of the community. In recent years more women are applying and being admitted than men. Then there is the question of background. Those with an upbringing in country areas can have an excellent range of experience and general knowledge of animal husbandry. Some of them may be the sons or daughters of farmers or vets. Clearly they have a lot to offer. Yet it would be unfair and divisive to fill a course with people who all had these advantages. What of the students coming from the cities where gaining practical experience is not so easy?

A few places will be kept for graduates taking veterinary science as a second degree. There will also be some places reserved for overseas students; they provide valuable income as well as added richness to the mix of students in the veterinary school. Nevertheless, the overwhelming majority of places on these courses will be filled by school-leavers or those who have taken a year out since leaving school.

Academic versus practical

As mentioned in Chapter 3, most of the veterinary schools require a minimum of six weeks' work experience made up in the way described above. However, despite the strong emphasis on practical experience demanded by all the veterinary schools, many people in the veterinary profession are concerned that the high A level grades required, currently ranging between A*AA and AAB, suggest that the profession is being filled with people who, while being academically very bright, are not so hot at dealing with the practical side of the work. Apart from the fact that it is often wrong to assume that academically able people are always very impractical, this trend reveals an imperfect understanding of the logistics of the UCAS operation each year and how the admissions tutors in the veterinary schools deal with it. The UCAS application and the supporting evidence of motivation are crucial to understanding what happens.

Professor Gaskell, when he was Dean of Liverpool's Veterinary School, left no room for doubt that the most important thing from the admissions point of view is understanding what the prospective student is about and his or her motivation. This has to come across in the student's UCAS application. But that is not to say that academic ability is unimportant. There is an enormous amount that has to be learned, and Professor Gaskell advises: 'It's the same with medicine – we find that A levels or their equivalent are good indicators of the ability to absorb, hold and recall information.'

The problem with weaker A levels is that you may start to find the amount of learning required difficult. Fortunately, veterinary medicine is in the position of being able to select the best of the most motivated applicants. It must be added that it is not in the interests of the profession, nor of the animals and owners whom the vets serve, to relax this strong position.

Admissions tests

Applicants to certain medicine, veterinary medicine and related courses are required to take the BioMedical Admissions Test (BMAT). The

BMAT is owned and administered by Cambridge Assessment, one of the world's largest assessment agencies. Time is the biggest factor in these admissions tests: there are a lot of questions and you don't have a lot of time to complete them. Of the seven UK veterinary schools, the test is currently required by Bristol, Cambridge and the RVC in London. The test takes place in November each year (you will need to check the BMAT website for the exact date) and in 2012 cost £42.50 for home and EU applicants and £72.50 for international applicants (you should check the website to get the most up-to-date costs). You sit the test at an examination centre, which is often your school, which will enter you for the test at your request. If you are not able to sit the test at your school, then you will have to find an external centre. Some centres charge an administration fee. There are three sections: Aptitude and Skills; Scientific Knowledge and Applications; and a Writing Task. Go to the website for more details (www.admissionstests.cambridgeassessment.org.uk/adt/bmat).

Have a go at the questions in the box below to give you an idea of the kind of things you will be asked.

Sample BMAT question

Doctors in Great Britain can work for the public health service, a commercial service, or both. Thirty per cent of doctors in Great Britain work, at least some of the time, for the commercial sector. On the basis of this information alone, deduce which of the following statements are true of doctors in Great Britain.

1   Some doctors work only in the public health service.
2   More doctors work in the public health service than the commercial sector.
3   Some doctors spend more time on commercial work than in the public health service.

   A 1 only
   B 2 only
   C 1 and 2 only
   D 2 and 3 only
   E 1, 2 and 3

Answer to sample question: C

Sample BMAT question

The UK government wishes to increase the number of young people from poorer families entering university education. However, it has recently changed the way in which it provides financial support for students. Whereas it used to provide grants that the student did not need to repay, it now provides loans that the student must repay when he or she enters employment. Research shows that students from poorer families are more likely to be deterred from going to university by the prospect of debt.

Which one of the following is an inference that can be drawn from the passage above?

A Students from poorer families are less interested in entering university.
B Universities will not be willing to help meet the government's target.
C The government's action is likely to deter poorer students from going to university more than richer.
D The prospect of debt is a deterrent to all students, not just the poorer ones.
E Maintenance grants were too expensive for the government to fund.

Answer to sample question: C

Sample BMAT question

At the end of daylight saving time, when clocks should be put back one hour, Julie puts hers forward one hour by mistake. Her friend Clare completely forgets about it and leaves hers unchanged. They had arranged to meet at 11a.m. the following day.

If neither realises her mistake before going to keep the appointment, what will happen?

A Julie arrives 2 hours after Clare
B Julie arrives 1 hour after Clare
C They arrive at the same time
D Julie arrives 1 hour before Clare
E Julie arrives 2 hours before Clare

Answer to sample question: D

From the specimen papers available on the Admissions Testing Service website (www.admissionstestingservice.org). Reprinted by permission of the University of Cambridge Local Examinations Syndicate.

Submitting your application

Applications for admission to veterinary science degree courses have to be made through UCAS Apply, the online UCAS system. The online UCAS form is accessed through the UCAS website (www.ucas.com). You register online either through your school or college, or as a private individual. Some of the information that you provide on the form is factual, such as where you live, where you have studied, what academic qualifications you have, details of examinations that you are going to take, and which university courses you are applying for. The final section on the form is the personal statement, where you write about why you want to study at veterinary school and about yourself. We will look at the personal statement in more detail in Chapter 6.

Once your form is complete, it is then accessed by the person who will write your reference; he or she then checks it, adds the reference and sends it to UCAS. After that, you can keep track of the responses from the universities using the online Track facility.

Applications for veterinary science must be received by UCAS by 15 October for entry in the following year. Applications received after this may be considered by the veterinary schools, but they are not bound to do so, and given the number of applications that they will receive, it is likely that they will not do so. In order to ensure that your application reaches UCAS by the deadline, you should complete it at least two weeks before this date so that your referee has time to write his or her report. The current UCAS application should be available via your school or college. However, if you have left school, or have any difficulties accessing the electronic application system, you should write, after 1 July in the year preceding entry, to UCAS, Rosehill, New Barn Lane, Cheltenham, Gloucestershire GL52 3LZ.

If you are applying to Cambridge, you are required to complete a Supplementary Application Questionnaire (SAQ), in keeping with the requirements of many other universities. More information on applications to Cambridge can be found in another book in this series, *Getting into Oxford & Cambridge*.

Application timeline

This timeline shows the tasks that you will need to be aware of over the course of your A level studies and gives an overview of the timing of some of the various things that you should plan for if you are to maximise your chances of gaining entry into a veterinary school.

Year 12

September: Now is the time to be getting work experience. In reality this should have started earlier than this point; however, there is still time and it should be continuous throughout the year in order to meet the criteria of the individual veterinary schools (see pages 27–28). This is a minimum requirement, so do not forget! The best advice is to get some work experience in every school holiday as well as some part-time weekend work in order to meet the requirements.

May/June: Do some serious thinking about the course you'd like to apply to. Get ideas from friends, relatives, teachers, books, etc. If possible, visit some campuses before you go away anywhere during the summer.

June/July: Make a shortlist of your courses.

August: Get your hands on some copies of the official and alternative (student-written) prospectuses, and departmental brochures for extra detail. They can usually be found in school or college libraries, but all the information can also be found by looking at university websites.

Year 13

September: Complete your application online and submit it to UCAS via a referee. It will be accepted from 1 September onwards.

15 October: Deadline for applying for places at veterinary school.

November: Universities hold their open days and sometimes interviews. Entrance examination for BMAT is held.

April: Universities begin to make their decisions and offers will be sent directly to you. If you are rejected by all of your choices, you can use UCAS Extra to look at other universities.

15 May: You must tell UCAS which offer you have accepted firmly and which one is your insurance choice. (The deadline is two weeks after the final decision you receive, if this falls earlier.)

Spring: Fill out yet more forms – this time for fees and student loans. You can get these forms from your school, college or local authority.

Summer: Sit your exams and wait for your results.

5 July: International Baccalaureate results.

5 August: Scottish Highers results.

16 August: When the A level results are published, UCAS will get in touch and tell you whether your chosen universities have confirmed your conditional offers. Do not be too disappointed if you have not got into your chosen institution; just get in touch with your school or college or careers office. Clearing is not likely to be an option for veterinary courses, although bioveterinary science may appear in August Clearing lists.

As you can see, your main task in your AS year is to start researching your courses and options, organising and carrying out work experience and then preparing your personal statement. The summer between your AS and A2 years should be used to continue building your work experience as well as registering and preparing for BMAT. In the second year, you must hit the ground running, because your UCAS application must be finished by early October and your BMAT will be on 7 November 2013. At the same time, you must also ensure that you stay on top of your studies so you maximise your chances of achieving the A grades you will need, and you should also start preparing for interview and practising your interview skills. Once your final exams are finished at the end of the year, it is simply a matter of waiting for your results so you can see whether you have secured a place.

How many applications to make

You may apply to only four veterinary science courses. If you apply to more than four, your UCAS application will be returned, and by the time you amend it, you may well have missed the 15 October deadline.

A common question is: 'Should I put a non-veterinary science choice in the remaining slot?' While universities cannot see which other courses you have applied to, there are arguments for and against applying to a non-veterinary science course, and you will need to discuss this with your careers adviser or referee. It would probably not be a good idea to apply for veterinary nursing, for example, but it might make sense to apply for a course in equine science. The main point to remember is that you can write only one personal statement and that needs to focus on what you ultimately want to study, veterinary science. This means it will be largely inappropriate for another subject and the admissions staff for that subject will see that you are really interested in veterinary science and so reject you from their course. The admissions staff at the veterinary schools cannot see your fifth choice and so, as long as you don't mention it in your personal statement, it will not affect their judgement. However, you should be wary of putting down a course that you are not interested in and you should try to put down only subjects that are closely related to veterinary science.

Therefore, holding 'insurance' offers will depend on how committed you are to veterinary science. An argument in favour of going all out for the total commitment of applying solely to veterinary schools is that if you fall short of the required grades, and have just missed out, you will almost certainly have the option of gaining entry into an alternative course through Clearing. This is because other pure and applied science courses are invariably much less competitive and you will be able to accept an offer if you want to do so, although it is more likely to be at a lower-ranked institution.

However, if you decide to choose an alternative course as your insurance choice, you should not put down medicine or dentistry. Although veterinary science admissions tutors would not automatically exclude anyone because of this mixture, they would certainly look long and hard for overwhelming evidence that veterinary science was what you really wanted. By the same token, you could hardly expect to satisfy the medical and dental admissions tutors!

All things being equal, it seems logical for applications that list clearly related subjects in the D sector of UCAS – the sector detailing all animal-related studies, such as agriculture, equine studies, animal physiology, biochemistry, microbiology and zoology – to possess that important quality of coherence and to fit in with the general thrust of your application.

A level predictions

As has already been indicated, performance in A levels (or equivalent exams) is not the sole determinant in selection because of the importance of other motivational factors. However, predicted A level performance is an important aspect for admissions tutors when sifting through and finding committed candidates likely to meet the stipulated academic level. Final decisions are made when A level results are known.

It is at this point that some rejected applicants will do better than predicted. When the admissions tutors learn that a rejected candidate has achieved top grades and is excellent in other respects, they have been known to change the original rejection to an unconditional acceptance for the following year. Over 100 places are settled each year in this way. Indeed, the majority of entrants to veterinary science courses will have taken a year out, whether they intended to or not. Those whose grades slip slightly below their conditional offer will usually be considered in August and could be offered entry if places are available. The importance, therefore, of A levels is that once the results are known, the tutors can announce the final decisions that have been made concerning the group of well-motivated and committed pre-selected candidates.

In certain cases, if applicants have met and exceeded the grades asked of them by a veterinary school, they are eligible to enter Adjustment through UCAS. However, it's extremely unlikely that the applicant would be able to find another course in veterinary medicine.

Case study

Twenty-year-old Joshua comes from Brighton and is now in the second year of his veterinary medicine course at the RVC. He decided to apply to the college having previously lived in London and knowing that he might want to live at, or near, home.

Joshua's ambition to be a vet is deep-rooted: 'From a young age, I knew I wanted to work with animals. We had a turtle, a dog, two cats and a parrot, a proper menagerie! I took an active interest in their welfare, which I know was "uncool" for a boy growing up! I also liked visiting farms. Luckily, for a city boy, I had an uncle who owned a farm in Bedfordshire so during my school holidays I would go and spend time there. I remember spending a couple of weeks there one summer and getting as involved as I could in some of the day-to-day farming chores, like milking and feeding. When I was 13 I got a part-time job at a local kennels and two years later a local vet invited me to spend time observing him at work during my school holidays. I'd written to him three times, so I think he knew I was serious and committed!

'I worked very hard for my GCSEs and A levels. I suppose I was lucky in the sense that I had an ambition driving me on. I was also extremely well aware of the importance of gaining really high grades at every opportunity. I studied Biology, Chemistry and Psychology to full A2 level and got two As and a B. Nothing gave me more pleasure up to that point than arriving at the Royal Veterinary College on my first day and knowing that this was the next step to achieving my goal of becoming a vet. Two years on, I'm loving it. I'm doing the course I've always wanted to do. I love working with animals and university life is brilliant. Definitely worth all the hard work!'

Once you have completed your application and you are totally happy with it you will need to complete the declaration – found under the 'Send to referee' section of Apply. UCAS cannot process your application unless you confirm your agreement with its terms and conditions, which legally binds you to make the required payment. Remember, by clicking the 'I agree' you are saying that the information you have provided is accurate, complete and all your own work and that you agree to abide by the rules of UCAS.

Referee's report

After you have completed the declaration, your application is ready to be passed to your referee for completion. He or she will then send it to UCAS. The referee is usually someone who knows you better than anyone else in your school or college, and someone who can draw on the opinions of other members of staff and on information contained in school records. In schools this is most likely to be your form tutor, whereas in colleges it will probably be your director of studies. However, mature students or graduates for whom school was too long ago for such a reference to be meaningful should approach people who know them well. A good idea is to consider asking someone for whom you have worked recently.

References are an important factor since they provide insight into your character and personality. They can also provide significant confirmation of career aims, achievements and interests. The referee's view of your abilities, in terms of analysis, powers of expression and willingness to question things, is the kind of independent information about you that will have an influence with selectors. Additional information about family circumstances and health problems, which candidates rarely offer about themselves, will also be taken into account.

Other supporting documentation

Because work experience in veterinary practices and farms is so important in the selection of applicants for veterinary school, you will be expected to list full details of all such experience. Some veterinary schools will send you a questionnaire asking you to expand on the information you gave about work experience in your UCAS application. Applicants can expect interested veterinary schools to follow up by writing to the veterinary practices and farms where you have worked for additional information about you (this information will be confidential). This is a good sign as it shows that your application has aroused more than a passing interest.

In essence, the veterinary school will ask whether the people you have worked with regard you as a suitable entrant into the veterinary profession. The sorts of issues that concern tutors are:

- general enthusiasm
- ability to express yourself clearly
- helpfulness
- practical ability
- attitude to the animals, to customers and to clerical and nursing staff in the practice – in other words, were you a pleasure to have around?

So, it is clear that the veterinary school can take steps to get hold of additional information about you. You can also help yourself by taking the initiative to gain documentary support. For example, once you have received your UCAS acknowledgement and application number, you can ask your local vet to write to the veterinary school(s) of your choice (quoting your application number), giving details of the work that you did there with extra details of any interesting cases with which you were involved. This information will go into your file and is bound to help, especially if the vet is able to say that he or she 'would like to see this person in veterinary school'.

There are exceptions to this arrangement. For instance, the RVC prefers that you bring copies of all supporting statements, references and casebooks to your interview rather than sending them in advance. It would therefore be wise to contact the individual schools to which you are applying to enquire whether they have any preference regarding how they receive additional statements supporting work experience.

Transferring from another degree

If you really want to become a veterinary surgeon, and with hard work you can attain the necessary academic standard, it is not a good idea to take a different degree. Some people are badly advised to do another degree and then try to transfer from another course into veterinary science. This is not feasible because it is necessary to study certain subjects that are exclusive to veterinary science from the beginning: examples are veterinary anatomy and ruminant physiology. In addition, the chance of there being extra places is remote. Transfer then becomes impossible and the only way you could proceed would be to go back and start your veterinary studies at the beginning. Therefore, no one should be advised to take a different course and then try to transfer. However, it is worth noting that Cambridge has been known to make some concessions to students wishing to transfer from mainly medically related degrees. Such students might, because of the Cambridge tripos system, be able to complete a veterinary science degree at the end of six or seven years' study, depending on when the transfer was made; but they will still need to study veterinary physiology and anatomy.

A further reason why it might prove unwise to do a degree in another subject is that, even if you become a graduate in another cognate subject, with a 2.i or even a First, your application could be assessed on the basis of your original A levels as well as on your subsequent university study. This is done in fairness to the large number of school-leavers applying.

A decisive argument against this route for most people is that, in nearly all cases, graduates in other subjects would be admitted only on a 'full cost' basis. Some colleges allocate a small number of places to graduates within the home and EU intake, but tuition fees for these would usually be at full cost payable throughout the course. There are no scholarships available for graduate applicants, with the possible exception of some Cambridge colleges or those that are privately funded.

Deferring entry and taking a gap year

The UCAS system permits you to apply at the start of Year 13 for entry a year after completion of your A levels. However, you will be expected to meet the conditions of the offer in the year of application. The majority of veterinary schools now welcome students deciding to postpone their entry to the course. The most common reasons given by students are the opportunity to travel, study or work abroad, or gain additional relevant experience for the course and profession they seek to enter. The latter reason is the one most likely to influence veterinary schools because many applicants do need to strengthen their range of relevant work experience. However, if you are thinking of this, it is better if you wait until you have got your A level grades and then apply in your gap year, as at that point you will have got more work experience, which ultimately is what you need to confirm to yourself that this is the right course.

You should be able to explain your plans for the year taken out. Does it involve some animal experience? Those coming from urban areas may find that undertaking a gap year of a relevant nature is slightly more difficult to achieve. It is a good idea to discuss this matter on an informal basis with an admissions tutor and get some advice.

What happens next?

About a week after UCAS receives your application, it will send you a welcome letter and an applicant welcome guide, confirming your personal details and choices. It is vital that you check this information carefully and inform UCAS if there are any inaccuracies. A common mistake is to select the foundation year rather than the start of the course proper, so make sure you haven't done this – for example, someone selecting veterinary medicine including a preliminary year (D104) at the University of Nottingham instead of veterinary medicine (D100) will have two options for a start date: the next academic year or the one after. Be alert and make sure you are selecting the next academic year unless you are taking a gap year or have been advised to do otherwise. Remember, you will be able to access your application at all times through the UCAS Track system using the same personal ID, username and password that you used to apply.

As soon as UCAS processes your application, your prospective universities can access it, but they will be unable to see the other courses and universities to which you have applied. Once a university has accessed your application, they may contact you to acknowledge receipt of your application; however, not all universities bother doing this, so don't worry if you don't hear from them initially.

The next stage is to wait to hear from the veterinary schools you applied to, once they have considered your application. If you are lucky, the veterinary schools will contact you, asking you to attend an interview. Most veterinary schools wait until all applications are in before deciding who to interview. It is not uncommon for students to hear nothing until after Christmas, so don't panic if you aren't contacted straight away.

If you are unlucky, you will receive a notification from UCAS telling you that you have been rejected by one or more of the veterinary schools. If this happens, don't despair: you may hear better news from another of the schools that you applied to. If you end up with four rejections, you should take the opportunity to carefully reassess whether veterinary medicine is a realistic career ambition for you and whether there were any parts of your application that let you down. If you still feel that veterinary medicine is for you, take the opportunity to strengthen any aspects of your application that were weak. Under no circumstances should you give up and decide that it is no longer worth working hard; this will only reduce your chances of making a successful application the following year.

Note that going through Clearing in August is not usually an option for entry into veterinary medicine. Places are limited and often oversubscribed – more offers are made than there are places available, even in a year when the fees increases have led to the government lifting the cap on university places. There can be the odd exception on a year-to-year basis when a few places are available; however, under no circumstances should you bank on any such places becoming available.

What to do if you are rejected

Generally, one of the main reasons for rejection is insufficient practical experience, particularly a lack of farm work. If this is true in your own case, you could try to remedy the deficiency between the A level examinations and the publication of the results. All applications are reconsidered after your A level results are known. If your academic results are satisfactory you may be offered a place for the subsequent year.

If you are rejected but have reached the necessary academic standard or have narrowly fallen short, you should think carefully before turning away from veterinary science, if that is really what you want to do. There are plenty of cases of people who have persisted and gained the extra practical experience that was needed to tip the scales in their favour. Determination to succeed is a quality that is generally recognised and supported. Think carefully before turning to another science subject. In most cases such a move will prove to be a decisive career choice. This is because it is not possible to transfer from another science course into veterinary school. Nor is it easy to take veterinary science as a second bachelor's degree: graduate applicants have to face stiffer competition and the prospect of having to pay high fees if accepted, as mentioned above.

6 | No one likes a copycat
The personal statement

Gone are the days of pen and paper. The personal statement is filled in using Apply, the online application system found on the UCAS website, so you can no longer rely on the size of your handwriting to cram in every last possible word. There is a 4,000-character limit (including spaces), which equates to roughly 47 lines. So remember, be concise in what you want to convey and try to be unique.

Importance of the personal statement

The personal statement may be the last part of the UCAS application you fill in, but it is certainly the most important and influential. Most of the information you supply via UCAS is a factual summary of what you have achieved, but in the personal statement you have your first chance to give expression, clarity and style to your application and hence bid for a place at veterinary school.

Make sure you plan your statement carefully. Remember that brevity can often produce a better, more directed answer. Word-process the statement first and then cut it down to within the maximum number of characters if necessary. Research shows that it is a good idea to structure your response. Consider using subheadings to give clarity for the busy admissions tutor, and make sure that the following points are covered in your personal statement.

- Why do you want to be a veterinary surgeon? There are many possible reasons and this is where your individuality will show.
- Outline your practical experience. Give prominence to the diverse nature of it, the clinics, farms, stables, etc. you have worked at or visited.
- Mention any specific interesting cases that you witnessed or assisted with.
- You like animals, but how do you respond to people?
- How did you get on with vets, nurses and the customers? Any teamwork experience?
- Give an indication of your career direction, even if it is tentative at this stage. Show that you have thought about the possibilities.

- Have you had any special achievements or responsibilities connected either with animals or with an outside interest?
- List other activities and interests of a social, cultural or sporting kind. Here is your chance to reveal more about yourself as an individual.
- Finally, remember to keep a copy of your personal statement before you pass it on to your referee. The copy will serve to refresh your memory before you are called for interviews.

The example personal statements below show how an applicant might structure their personal statement. The first example illustrates an old-fashioned but methodical approach to writing a personal statement and will always be useful as a template for your own statement. The other examples are different in their own ways: for instance, the second focuses primarily on work experience, whereas in the third, as well as detailing their work experience, the applicant has also shown an appreciation of different issues affecting vets in practice today.

It is impossible to pick one of these personal statements as the definitive article because they are all individual. There are no right or wrong answers, only a correct template or model to use. As long as the personal statement is personal and means something to you, you will have achieved your goal.

Quotes are desirable in a personal statement only if you can link them to the point that you are trying to make.

Remember: be concise and try to be unique.

Example personal statement 1 (3,987 characters with spaces)

Studying anthropology at university gave me the benefit of an amalgamation of arts and sciences, which has given me the confidence to take on the science A levels which I am currently studying. It was whilst competing in hunter jumpers at school that my involvement with horses, both competitive and pastoral, kindled in me the desire to pursue veterinary medicine, as I was exposed to their injuries at an early age. I also volunteered at the Pegasus Riding for the Disabled programme in Connecticut. The experience enabled me to interact with children with severe disabilities and see the positive effect the horses had on them. During my adolescence, I was involved with the care of a pack of French boarhounds in Burgundy. The management of a large group of canines was different from the care of domestic dogs and raised my interest in the ethical issues surrounding hunting. I witnessed a different side of veterinary care, this time of working animals. The pack's behaviours and needs were drastically different from what I had learned to expect. They were frequently injured and were cared for on-site. On one occasion a hound was lacerated during a hunt and the wound was sutured by one of the caretakers with my assistance. The physical demands of restraining a large, distressed animal made me consider the physical demands of the job in the face of a difficult patient.

After leaving school I worked as a stable manager and riding instructor in Zambia, managing a yard of over sixty horses, many of them previously abandoned and mistreated. Their needs were different from those of the healthy working horses under my care and I was fortunate to have the support of a knowledgeable and reassuring veterinarian, a quality which is as important in a vet as clinical ability. I was able to assist on a Caesarean section, something which I was very curious to witness. Whilst on intermission from my degree I spent 10 weeks at Hagyard Equine Hospital in Kentucky as a veterinary assistant. One night an emergency call brought a pregnant mare in distress, initially attributed to colic. However, an ultrasound revealed a large tumour. The owners requested the surgery despite the difficulties involved due to the horse's value. The importance of profit margins in decision-making was something I hadn't considered prior to that event but it became apparent to me that in equine medicine, surgical intervention is often a case of saving the breeding potential of a horse, rather than improving quality of life. Despite the financial motivations of many horse owners in pursuing expensive surgeries, there were other occasions which showcased the professionalism and commitment of the surgeons. I was able to participate in numerous colic surgeries during which horses were saved. The willingness of the vets to come out for emergencies in the middle of the night with good humour made me more aware of the commitment necessary to be a good vet as well as the ongoing demands of emergency medicine. My experiences working with vets have shown me some of the skills which I believe to be necessary to the career: empathy, calm, reassurance and understanding. I believe that I am already strong in these areas, and I hope that this, coupled with my enormous passion for animal welfare, as well as my desire to learn, will go some of the way to making me a good vet.

I am currently reading about the chronic inbreeding in purebred dogs, particularly the study undertaken by Imperial College to determine the genetic variance of certain breeds. Additionally, I have been following the creation of a veterinary tissue bank in the UK with great interest. Away from my studies, I have been a keen swimmer, having started in New York when hunter jumping was not an option. I still swim on a regular basis in London, as well as undertaking endurance in Canada every year. I trained as a singer from the age of 9 and concentrated on opera when I reached 16. I continue to enjoy opera regularly.

Notes on personal statement

- Makes good comparisons between different treatments of animals.
- Considers the physical demands of the course.
- Considers ethical issues surrounding finances.
- Gives a little context about herself.

However:

- Imbalanced and tends to focus purely on horses.
- Words such as 'love' and 'passion' are not recommended.

Example personal statement 2 (3,277 characters with spaces)

It is my commitment to animal welfare that attracted me to veterinary science and made me keen to further develop my knowledge of animal physiology and psychology.

I currently work part-time at a local veterinary practice. I am involved in the complete process from administering treatment for a sick animal to its recovery and aftercare. There are many tension-filled moments as the vet begins treatment on a gravely sick animal and I have had the opportunity to help in counselling grief-stricken owners who are facing the loss of their beloved pets. It takes great care and sensitivity and I clearly observed this during a work experience placement at an animal home, where I had the opportunity of shadowing a vet in the operating theatre.

I am now a regular volunteer at Mayhew Animal Home where there are kennels and a cattery. I have also spent a day in a large 24-hour veterinary hospital and embarked on a veterinary course with Nottingham University (Vetsim) in the summer of 2011. This was followed by a similar course on a dairy farm sponsored by the Royal Veterinary College. I also gained experience on an organic dairy farm in Devon where I observed Holstein milking cows and poultry. I was informed about the oestrus cycle and the different breeds. I watched the removal of a hernia from a calf.

I also had a work experience placement on Harrow Boys School Farm where I worked with sheep, long-horned cows and donkeys. I was involved in many different activities from herding sheep to helping transport them from field to field and putting up electric fences. I also had a brief stint on Heathrow Special Needs Farm where I worked with ponies, goats, rabbits and chickens.

One of my most interesting placements was at Ridgeway Stables. In just a few weeks I learnt a vast amount about horses in terms of grooming, basic anatomy and general welfare. I learnt about the role of horses for work and pleasure. I also assumed a position of responsibility since I was allocated small groups of children to show around the stables and educate them on the different horse colours/breeds and teach them basic grooming techniques.

I have strong interpersonal skills and I believe that the ability to empathise with people is an important quality for a career in this field. I have participated in a variety of community activities, such as fundraising and mentoring younger students at school. I have also done charity work abroad with a charity for homeless orphans in Sierra Leone, West Africa. All these experiences have brought me into contact with people from all walks of life and I am able to respond to sensitive situations with a calm approach.

I am studying biology and chemistry, which will enhance my analytical and practical skills in the veterinary field. I have gained further knowledge by watching documentaries on the natural world. I have read James Herriot and Gerald Durrell and can relate to the humorous mishaps that come with a profession when dealing with animals.

I wish to pursue a career in this field as I believe I have strong problem-solving skills in this dynamic and unpredictable area of animal science and care. I have an intellectual curiosity and strength that will help find creative solutions for animals and achieve my career ambitions.

Notes on personal statement

- Good ongoing work experience.
- Includes a variety of activities.
- Talks about specifics.

However:

- Introduction needs to say when this commitment started.
- A little too narrative.
- Needs to pick out how the experiences differ and what was learned on work experiences.
- Should talk about the differences of working with large animals.
- Reading needs to be developed to give a more observed remark.

Example personal statement 3 (3,965 characters with spaces)

I knew before secondary school that I wanted to be a vet and when I started doing a variety of work experience and pre-vet courses I began to see how much would be involved – hence my work experience blog: in_vet_erate@livejournal.com. When my two-year-old guinea pig developed a growth I became intrigued by the vet and all he had to say. My work experience began there when I was 14: first during the school holidays, then a three-week summer job in 2009, when I was trusted to restrain animals while the vet took blood, gave injections and inserted catheters. I have had ongoing paid work there as a weekend kennel hand since January 2010, going in when they are closed to feed and, if necessary, medicate boarding cats. Other vet experience includes a week at a rural small-animal practice and four days with a large-animal vet. Highlights for me in these contexts were correctly recognising a case of feline diabetes and being guided to perform rectal examinations on several cows.

Two days at an abattoir showed me aspects of the meat industry. It provided an excellent anatomy lesson and a glimpse into pathology. Three days at a vet laboratory gave a different slant on this and I learned to do blood smears and separate serum from blood.

I have had varied farm experience: two weeks on a dairy farm, two days of lambing and a week at a large pig farm. On these farms I delivered lambs, drenched them, gave bottle feeds and docked tails, and with the pigs I gave injections, cut teeth and performed AI on several sows. Even more interesting was working for a week on a buffalo farm (herd of 200). I was intrigued by these more 'wild', less domesticated animals and that consequently mastitis and digital dermatitis are less common. I was very involved in all the tasks in the milking parlour, including giving oxytocin injections.

I attended Vetsim and Vet-Medlink, VetCam and VetQuest, the Embryo Vet School course and 'An Introduction to Farm Animal Management' at Harper Adams UC. These courses linked satisfyingly with my work experience where I saw theory in practice. They were a fascinating glimpse into the diversity and challenge of veterinary medicine and I have been eager to go on all I could. Completing an ILM Level 2 course in Effective Team Member Skills at school made me more aware of effective team working both on farms and in vet surgeries. On Bronze and Silver Duke of Edinburgh expeditions I enjoyed the humour and support that comes from teamwork and on work experience I enjoyed pulling together to milk a large herd and for a busy night of lambing.

I relish challenges: I enjoy grappling with a problem and gain immense satisfaction when I arrive at a solution. Developing skills is also satisfying: playing the violin and recorder to Grade 8 (increasing my motor skills); being logical and methodical with maths but also open to the possibility of a solution sliding out of the blue. History has improved my academic skills of essay writing and being analytical. In chemistry there is the problem-solving factor and also interesting chemical processes, such as homeostasis. I especially enjoy biology and have completed papers on bluetongue disease and also, from an extra day at Vet-Medlink, a paper on nanotechnology which I passed with merit.

Responsibilities at school that tie into my interests include helping the junior school orchestra and volunteering as a student librarian. I love to read, whether novels or the Veterinary Practice journal – the articles detailing procedures are particularly fascinating and may be useful in the future. I also enjoy ballet and tennis, learning Mandarin and cross-stitch, which will hopefully be useful for suturing.

I am very self-motivated with a great enthusiasm for veterinary science. The opportunity to work with a vast range of species and the numerous skills that are required as a vet are prospects that I find very exciting and I eagerly look forward to the challenges I will face.

Notes on personal statement

- Includes a reference to the student's blog – admissions tutors do say to include a link to a blog (if you have one) if you want a way to provide them with more information.
- Some good examples are given.
- Talks about current studies.
- Mention of some manual dexterity.

However:

- Mentions a lot of work experience but not much depth to the discussion about it.
- Could include more detail on the Vetlink courses.

Example personal statement 4 (3,974 characters with spaces)

From a young age I have had a deep interest in animals, which was encouraged by my holiday job on a poultry farm since 2003, yet it was not until recently that I seriously considered veterinary science to be a viable career option. Throughout my time at school I was guided towards engineering; however, I was never really certain that it was what I wanted to do. I therefore rejected my five engineering offers part way through my gap year, in order to apply for veterinary science.

During my gap year I worked with a wild game vet in South Africa, on private game farms and hunting lodges all over the country, capturing, transporting and supervising the general care of the animals. As a result of this I began for the first time to look at becoming a vet. Upon my return to the UK I began a week's work experience with my local vets in Sussex in order to investigate the more typical side of veterinary work. It was invaluable to be able to see the day-to-day side of veterinary work. This ranged from small-animal surgery to dealing with some of the more difficult clients. One incident that stands out was an eye enucleation, my first real experience of surgery. Aside from the fascinating surgery, it was wonderful to see the dog a few days later, once the swelling had subsided, and he was returning to normal. I also accompanied vets on their large-animal visits, helping with tuberculosis testing and debudding in cattle, and attempting a few pregnancy diagnoses of my own. It was interesting to see the differences in approach between working with animals in the UK and in South Africa: in general I found that in the UK the processes of diagnosis and treatment had a much greater emphasis on science, as opposed to the 'patch and go' system when working with wild game. I have been able to continue working there over the last few months. Alongside this, I have worked on a dairy farm, in a stable and an animal rescue sanctuary. On the dairy farm I worked as a labourer and was involved in all aspects of farm work, from mucking out to milking. I learnt a great deal while I was there, in particular relating to the prevention and treatment of mastitis and milk fever, which I was surprised to see being carried out by the farmers, rather than the vets, illustrating the practical rather than theoretical side to the treatment. My week at the stables was brilliant; I arrived with very little experience of horses, and after that week I now feel confident in horse handling. It was a busy week, with visits from the vet, the farrier and the dentist, and I watched them all with interest. Especially noteworthy was a case of thrush that developed from a split in the frog of a shire horse, and as my week came to an end we could see a decrease in lameness. As a result of this work experience I am now absolutely certain that veterinary science is the career path that I wish to follow.

I was awarded a prestigious Army 6th Form Scholarship in 2005, securing a place at Sandhurst upon the completion of my studies. I was also the head of the Combined Cadet Force and I regularly return as a Civilian Instructor. Through the CCF I won a Gliding Scholarship from the RAF, achieving my solo wings, and I was invited back to train as an instructor. At school I was a prefect, and also competed in school and house rugby matches. I am a keen rock climber, and have completed two Army training courses, as well as climbing with the school.

I am now studying for two A levels in Biology and Chemistry in London, and alongside this I am continuing my work at my local vets in Sussex. Over my Christmas break I have also arranged some work experience at the Heathrow Airport Animal Reception Centre, which will show me some of the problems faced when transporting animals around the world, and also introduce me to the vaccines and documents required to do so. As well as this I am going to Wales to help with Christmas lambing, as preparation for the Sussex lambing season.

Notes on personal statement

- Variety of work experience.
- Good examples given.
- Talks about work experience to be done – this can also be a negative as universities require you to have done it already.

However:

- Not enough depth to experiences.
- Too narrative.
- Unclear as to what sparked the move from engineering. On the one hand there is mention of an interest in animals from a young age and on the other it was feeling suffocated by others.
- In some ways too much gap filling, which is evident as there is not too much work experience to rely on.

Bear in mind that the clever personal statements will look at the course requirements, which are roughly the same for different universities (see pages 35–37), and discuss them in the personal statement.

7 | So why did the chicken cross the road?
The interview

When the veterinary schools have received the UCAS applications, they will sift through them and decide who to call for interview. Only approximately one in three applicants to each institution will get an interview, but this can vary from year to year and between universities.

Don't be afraid of the big bad interviewer. They will huff and puff but if you make your house out of bricks you will remain firm and resolute in your interview.

Timing

The timing of interviews can be anything from November to March, so some candidates have to wait some time before getting their interview, and because of this timescale some candidates will get a late decision. The Cambridge colleges usually conduct their interviews in December, along with those for other courses at the university.

The purpose of the interview

The interview is designed to find out more about you. In particular, the interviewers (possibly a panel) will want to satisfy themselves about your motivation and the extent of your commitment to becoming a qualified veterinary surgeon, and so they may ask you about the following areas.

- Have you an appropriate attitude towards animal welfare?
- Are you reasonably well informed about the implications of embarking on a veterinary career?
- Are you a mature person possessing a balanced outlook on life?
- Will they be satisfied that you have the ability to cope with the pace of what is generally acknowledged to be a long and demanding course?

To help them they will have your UCAS application, your referee's report and any supporting statements made by veterinary practitioners or people for whom you have worked. They will already have a good idea of your academic ability.

Preparation

Experience shows that personal qualities are just as important as academic ability, perhaps more so. The way you come across will be influenced by how confident you are. This does not mean being overconfident. Many people believe that they can get through interviews by thinking on their feet and taking each question as it comes. This is probably an unwise attitude. Good preparation is the key. By being well informed on a variety of issues you will be able to formulate answers to most questions. There will always be the unexpected question for which no amount of preparation can help, but you can minimise the chance of this happening.

Confidence based on good preparation is the best kind. It is not the puffed-up variety that can soon be punctured by searching questions. While it is true that the interviewers will want to put you at your ease and will try to make the atmosphere informal and friendly, there is no doubt that for you there will be some tension in the situation. Think positively – this may be no bad thing. Many of us perform better when we are on our toes.

Some schools will be able to offer you a mock interview. Sometimes they can arrange for a person from outside the school to give the interview, which can help make it feel more realistic. If you are not sure about whether this facility is available, ask your school careers department. They will be keen to help if they can.

If you know anyone, student or staff, connected with one of the veterinary schools, ask for their advice. They may be able to give you an idea of what to expect. Start your preparation by looking at your copy of the personal statement you submitted to UCAS. This is the most important part of your UCAS application and it should tell the interviewers a lot about you as a person, your work experience, your interests and skills. Many of the questions they ask will be prompted by what you have written in it. The questions will most likely begin with those designed to put you at your ease. As the interview proceeds you should expect them to become more searching. Try practising your answers to questions like those shown below:

Question: *Did you have any trouble getting here?*

Comment: This is the sort of friendly question that is meant to get you started. Do not spend too long on it, but take the opportunity to be sociable, try to relax – and smile.

Question: *Have you visited here before?*

Comment: Did you go to the open day? If so, this is the moment to mention the fact. The interviewer will almost certainly follow up and ask what you thought of it. The faculty probably invested a lot of time and work in preparing it, so go easy on criticism! However, you should be prepared to say what you found was helpful and informative. It is then easier to make an additional constructive criticism. Bear in mind that the interviewers will expect you to have done your homework. If you hope to spend the next five or six years of your life at that institution, you should certainly have made efforts to see whether it is the right place for you. Although your choice is limited to four out of seven veterinary schools, you still have a choice to make. If you answer, 'No, but I've heard that you have a good reputation,' you are hardly likely to convince them that you really want to go there. Similarly, answering, 'No, but I think that all of the veterinary schools are pretty similar' will not enhance your chances.

Question: *What did you think of our brochure?*

Comment: This is an alternative opening question on which you may have an opinion. Some veterinary schools, such as London, have their own brochure; others have entries in the main prospectus. Be prepared: show that you have at least read it and have an opinion. You could say: 'I thought that it was very informative about the structure of the course, and I particularly liked the case histories of your students – they made me realise that students in a similar situation to me can get a place.' Hopefully, this will lead to a question which will allow you to talk about your experience.

Question: *How do you think you are doing with your A levels?*

Comment: This is not a time for modesty. You would not be having this interview if your school had not predicted that you will get good results. You should be sounding optimistic while at the same time indicating that you are working hard. They may also be interested to learn what your favourite subjects are, so be ready for a follow-up question along those lines. If you have a good set of AS results, you could mention them at this point. You could also talk about a biology project that was relevant to veterinary science. As with the two previous examples, your aim should be to steer these rather boring questions towards topics that you have prepared and that will show you in the strongest light.

Question: *What do you think of the TV programmes about vets?*

Comment: Nowadays, programmes specifically about vets in the UK are seen as less marketable than programmes such as those documenting wildlife abroad or those featuring celebrities such as Sir David Attenborough: human nature is such that people are more interested by the exotic or the unknown. A few years ago there were several programmes on television following the everyday work of a vet. Such programmes were not always good for the professional standing of the vet. They made entertaining television, especially when they showed the animals and the caring 'honest broker' role of the vet between animals and humankind. They also almost universally presented vets as amiable people. On the other hand, though, you could argue that veterinary science was undermined when the programmes degenerated into 'soaps', with a portrayal of young vets whose work was an easy or incidental part of their lives. In your answer, show that you have thought about television's influence.

Question: *Why do you want to study veterinary science?*

Comment: The direction of the interview can change quite suddenly. Be ready for the switch in questioning; the answer will bring into focus your attitude to animals, the range of your work experience, those important manual skills, and your commitment to all the hard work entailed in studying to become a qualified professional veterinary surgeon admitted to the register of the RCVS. This is your opportunity, if you have not already done so, to mention your work experience, and to emphasise how your determination to become a vet increased as a result. This is an important question and needs a full answer, but keep your reply to less than two minutes. Practise this. Remember that research findings show that if you exceed two minutes you risk boring your listeners.

Question: *Why do you want to come to this veterinary school?*

Comment: This is a natural follow-up question, so be prepared for it. The answer is personal to you: you may want to go to a new area of the country; you may know the area well because you have relations living there; your local vet may have recommended this particular veterinary school to you; the reputation of the school may have impressed you because of some particular specialty in which you are also interested. There could be several reasons, but make sure you give an honest answer, not just what you think the interviewer wants to hear.

Question: *Tell us something about your work experience with animals.*

Comment: This is one of the big questions of the interview. It would be surprising if the interviewers do not already have feedback from where you have been working. The interviewers will know what happens in a veterinary practice or on a farm, so lists of things that you saw or did will not shed any light on your suitability for the profession. Instead, concentrate on your reactions to the experience. Did you enjoy it? Were there any interesting or unusual cases that stick in your memory? Is your enthusiasm clear? Do you show your respect and sympathy for the animals? And what about the people – did you get on with them? The key phrases here are 'For example, when I . . .' and 'For instance, I was able to . . .'

Question: *What are the main things you learned from your work experience?*

Comment: This is the typical follow-up question that gives you a chance to summarise and underline your impressions. You could try to indicate the varied nature of your experience and the different types of practice or farms you saw. There is also the business side of working with animals, for which you may not originally have been prepared. Maybe you were astonished at the responsibilities of the veterinary nurses. Be prepared to intrigue your listeners. A related question is: 'From your work experience, what do you think are the qualities necessary to be a successful vet?' Rather than answering 'Stamina, communication, physical fitness, problem-solving . . .' and so on, bring in examples of things that you saw. For example: 'The ability to solve problems. For instance, when I accompanied a vet to a riding school, it was clear that one of the horses was very distressed, but it was unclear why . . .' and then go on to explain the steps involved in the diagnosis and treatment.

Question: *Have you ever felt frightened of animals?*

Comment: Vets shouldn't be frightened of animals, particularly small ones! However, honesty compels most of us to admit that we have at times and in certain situations felt vulnerable to a kick or bite. Explain the situation and what was said at the time – vets are noted for their humour!

Question: *What do you think of rearing animals for meat?*

Comment: This type of question might be asked because it checks on your motivation. Perhaps you should start by looking at it from the animal's viewpoint. Animals should be kept well, with good standards of husbandry, and eventually slaughtered humanely. Of course, the animal does not know the reason for its being slaughtered, but you do. Some of your future clients may be farmers who make their living from supplying meat or poultry – what is your reaction? If you oppose eating meat, you should be honest but make it clear that you would be able to remain professional.

Question: *How do you feel about cruelty to animals?*

Comment: With the strong interest in and liking for animals that you would expect from all veterinary students, they will be watching your reaction. This is a question that you should expect and your response, while putting animal welfare first, should be strong and well reasoned rather than too emotional. What would you do if you thought a farmer was acting in a cruel way to some of his livestock? Go to the police straight away? Talk over the difficulty with a colleague? Threaten the farmer by mentioning that you might bring in the RSPCA? The interviewers are not expecting you to come up with a perfect answer but rather to show that you are capable of coming up with a well-balanced and reasoned solution.

Question: *What are your views on euthanasia?*

Comment: They are looking for your ability to balance an argument. Any relevant examples would be helpful. Talk about it from the point of view of the animal and the owner. Do not be concerned about your own feelings as this is the job you wish to do and this is a regrettable part of it. Think of it from a humane point of view versus a human response. Also consider the implication of putting a horse down at the races (the Grand National for example) as there are obviously financial issues at play as well.

Question: *How important is the business element of veterinary medicine?*

Comment: Remember, some vets have to be businesspeople as well. Smaller practices rely on the vets themselves to manage the practice. Therefore you must be prepared to be strong when asking people for money, even in the face of tragedy for them. That can be hard but the practice's survival is mostly based on your ability to recoup your charges.

There will, of course, be questions on your scientific knowledge and current topics (listed on pages 70–88). Be prepared to answer many different types of questions.

> Remember: good preparation is the key.

Importance of the interview

These are just a few of the possible questions and issues that you might expect to come up at a selection interview for entry to veterinary school. To be called for interview is a positive sign as it indicates that your application is being considered, and a good interview can lead to an offer. Another reason for trying to do well at the interview stage is that candidates whose grades fall just below those required in their conditional offers are often reconsidered. If places are available, a good interview performance could tip the balance in your favour.

Demeanour

Most candidates will do their best to prepare well for the interview by anticipating likely questions. However, very few candidates realise that the visual impression they are creating will count for as much as their verbal answers to questions. It is a bit like the old saying, 'It's not what you say it's the way that you say it.'

Admissions tutors are unlikely to admit that they are going to be influenced by appearance and body language, but they are only human. There is bound to be subjectivity involved. What can you do about it? Try to look your best and try to be as relaxed as possible in what will seem to be a fairly tense situation. Here are a few points to watch.

Body language

When you first enter the room, smile and give a firm handshake. Veterinary schools are friendly places and like to exude informality. Sit comfortably and reasonably upright, leaning forward slightly. This position makes you look and feel alert. Try not to be so tense that you are crouching forward, giving an impression of a panther about to spring. Do not go to the other extreme of leaning back and looking irritatingly self-assured. Where do you put your hands during the interview? Try resting one on top of the other on your lap. Alternatively, let each hand rest by your side. It is not a good idea to have your arms folded – it looks as though you are shutting the interviewer out.

Speak clearly and deliberately. Do not rush things. When people are nervous they tend to speed up, which makes it harder for the listener. Make eye contact – looking at the person who asked you the question. If it is a panel interview, let your glance take in others at the table, to make them feel that they are included. You should certainly have at least one mock interview, which, if possible, should be recorded on video so that you can see how you come across. You will then be able to spot any mannerisms, such as touching your head or cracking your knuckles, which might distract the interviewers.

Your appearance

Look your best. This does not mean that you should look like a tailor's dummy, but you should wear clothes that are smart, not showy, and in which you feel comfortable. Pay attention to details such as polishing your shoes and washing your hair.

Case study

Richard sat his A levels last year, and is in his first year studying veterinary science in Scotland. Richard was brought up in London, but his family moved to Essex at the start of his final year of GCSEs. Richard had wanted to be a vet since the age of 11, when his school went on a visit to London Zoo and were allowed behind the scenes and given a talk by a vet who worked there. 'We had always had pets at home, including cats, dogs and various small animals and birds. At times, home was like an animal sanctuary as my mother was always looking after neighbours' pets. To be honest, I found them all a bit boring, and it was only the visit to the zoo that made me sit up and realise that being a vet involved more than putting down sick animals or vaccinating them when they were young.'

The change of school disrupted Richard's studies. Having been on target for A and A* grades at his previous school, he managed to gain only two A grades. 'Under the old A level system I would have been in trouble because I would have been judged only on my GCSE grades and A level predictions, but mine was the first year to sit AS levels, and I was determined to do well as I knew that if I did, I could show that my GCSE grades were not a true reflection of my ability. I took Biology, Chemistry, Maths and Psychology and got A grades in each one. I then carried on with Biology, Chemistry and Maths and got AAA. I had two interviews, and got an offer from the first one. I was probably overconfident in the second interview, since I already knew I had an offer, but I was surprised to be rejected. Luckily, I got the grades that I needed and so didn't need an insurance offer.'

Richard started getting work experience in the summer following his GCSE examinations. He worked for three weeks on a local farm 'mainly painting fences, but also being able to feed the cattle and help with milking', and spent a further week on another farm near Edinburgh where his uncle lived. 'That is why I decided that I wanted to study in Scotland – not only because I liked the area, but also I thought that I would have an advantage over other applicants since I had worked there.' The following summer, Richard spent two weeks with a vet in a nearby town, mainly concentrating on domestic pets, and a further week with the vet who visited the farm in Scotland. 'I was lucky – my school helped me to organise the first placement with a vet, and my cousin was already shadowing the Scottish vet and she asked him if I could come along. The irony was that I got a place and she didn't! Luckily, she now has an offer for next year but at a different veterinary school.'

Topical and controversial issues

Your interviewer will want to find out whether you are genuinely interested in the profession, and alongside work experience, this includes testing your knowledge, awareness and appreciation of important issues: after all, if you are planning to devote the next 40 or so years of your life to veterinary science, you ought to be interested in issues that affect the profession.

Most interviews last only 15 to 20 minutes, so there may not be time for questions of a more topical or controversial nature. Nevertheless, it may be worth investing a little thought into how you might sketch out an answer to questions covering one or more of the following issues, each of which will be outlined at the end of this chapter:

- avian influenza (bird flu)
- bovine tuberculosis and badgers
- bluetongue disease
- canine influenza
- methicillin-resistant *Staphylococcus aureus* (MRSA)
- foot-and-mouth disease
- bovine spongiform encephalopathy (BSE)
- animal obesity
- canine lungworm
- High Profile Breed List for dogs
- Schmallenberg virus
- swine influenza virus
- intensive farming
- fox hunting
- fall of dairy prices
- Dangerous Dogs Act
- hybrid dogs
- animal testing.

Remember, most of the time there is no right or wrong answer for questions relating to issues such as these. It is really a case of demonstrating your understanding of an issue, your quality of judgement and your ability to discuss the issue clearly, logically and succinctly. A burst of enthusiasm and conviction won't do any harm either.

It goes without saying that the more informed you are, the more realistic your chance of entering this profession, so keeping up to date with recent developments affecting the veterinary profession is not only important but compulsory. The best sources of information are the broadsheet newspapers and internet news websites such as that of the British Veterinary Association (BVA: www.bva.co.uk). As well as the news sections, the health sections contain articles that will be of interest.

Read a newspaper every day, cut out or photocopy articles of interest, and keep them in a scrapbook so that you can revise from them before your interview. You will also find the Defra website (www.defra.gov.uk) extremely helpful. Other useful websites are listed in Chapter 12.

Questions on these issues are your chance to display a depth of knowledge from which you can open a discussion and show the clarity of analytical thought needed to be a vet. In many ways it is symptomatic of the profession and therefore good preparation. Good research ahead of your interview will also give you the confidence to feel able to discuss these issues with a professional.

At the time of going to print, the issues below are the most important current topics affecting the industry within recent years.

Avian influenza (bird flu)

The first human case of avian influenza or bird flu was in Hong Kong in 1997. Before then it wasn't known that this type of illness could be passed from birds directly to humans. The virus is spread when infected birds excrete the virus in their faeces. Once this dries it becomes a powder and is therefore easily inhaled. Symptoms are similar to other types of flu – fever, malaise, sore throat and coughing. People can also develop conjunctivitis. All 18 people infected in 1997 had been in close contact with live birds in markets or on farms.

Countries known to have been affected by the disease include Cambodia, Indonesia, South Korea, China, Japan, Thailand, Vietnam and Hong Kong. Furthermore, since January 2004, human cases of avian influenza have been reported in Asia, Africa, the Pacific region and Europe. Avian flu has been seen to have a high fatality rate in humans. In 1997, six out of the 18 people who were infected died. In an outbreak in 2004, there were over 20 confirmed deaths.

There are 15 different strains of the virus, but it is the H5N1 strain that infects humans and causes high death rates. Even within the H5N1 strain, however, variations are seen, and slightly different strains are being seen in the different countries where there have been outbreaks of the disease. The H5N1 virus that emerged in Asia in 2003 continues to evolve and may adapt so that other mammals may be susceptible to infection as well. Moreover, it is likely that H5N1 infection among birds has become endemic in certain areas and that human infections resulting from direct contact with infected poultry and/or wild birds will continue to occur. So far, the spread of the H5N1 virus from person to person has been rare and limited.

Patients suffering from avian flu are being treated with antiviral drugs while researchers continue to work to develop a vaccine. In 2004, the EU announced that it was considering a precautionary ban on the importation of poultry meat and products from Thailand. At the same time, millions of birds were culled in an attempt to stop the spread of the disease among birds, which would in turn prevent it being passed on to humans. Currently, there is a ban on the importation of birds and bird products from H5N1-affected countries. The regulation states that no person may import or attempt to import any birds, whether dead or alive, or any products derived from birds (including hatching eggs), from the specified countries.

In January 2006, two children from the eastern Turkish town of Dogubeyazit, whose family kept poultry at their home, died having contracted the virulent H5N1 strain. Three months later, in the Scottish town of Fife, tests confirmed that a swan there had died from the deadly H5N1 strain of the avian flu virus. The discovery made Britain the fourteenth country in Europe to have the disease in its territory. The first major outbreak in the UK was in February 2007, on a turkey farm in Suffolk. There have been further such instances, the latest one being in Oxfordshire, where the highly pathogenic H7N7 strain – a subtype of the species influenza A virus – was found in laying hens. In November 2008, the UK became free from avian influenza as defined by the rules of the World Organisation for Animal Health (OIE). The last reported case in the United Kingdom was in 2009. As of January 2012, the World Health Organization (WHO) confirmed that avian influenza has led to 344 deaths.

Bovine tuberculosis and badgers

Bovine tuberculosis (bTB) is a serious disease in cattle. Although the risk of tuberculosis spreading to humans through milk or meat is slight, it can be transmitted through other means, particularly to farm workers who have direct contact with the animals. The number of cattle slaughtered because of bTB increased from 599 in 1986 to 22,570 in 2004. In 2008 the number was roughly 40,000 and in January to March 2009 there was a 20% rise on the same period in 2008. The National Farmers' Union (NFU) has estimated that the cost in compensation to British farmers could easily reach £1 billion by 2013.

There is uncertainty about the cause of the spread of bTB in cattle, but many people believe that it is passed on by badgers – a protected species. There is widespread support within the farming community for the culling of badgers, but this is opposed by wildlife and conservation groups. In 1998 the government set up a badger-culling trial as well as taking steps to test the carcasses of badgers killed on the roads (about 50,000 every year) in order to try to find out more about the causes of the disease in cattle. However, the results were inconclusive, and the two opposing sides in the argument are still at loggerheads: the fundamental question remains unanswered – is bTB spread from badgers to cattle, from cattle to badgers, or is other wildlife involved?

In November 2004, the government introduced enhanced testing and control measures to help improve the detection of bTB, so that action could be taken quickly to prevent the spread of the disease. A 10-year government strategic framework for the sustainable control of bTB in Great Britain was published in March 2005. Through this framework, the government aims to bring about a sustainable improvement in control of bTB by 2015. In December 2005, the government also announced pre-movement testing in England and Wales to help reduce the risk of bTB spreading between herds.

According to recent data, there was a reduction in the number of new bTB incidents in 2005 and again in 2006. Despite this reduction, however, levels of bTB remain high in comparison with other EU countries. On 7 July 2008, Hilary Benn MP, the then Secretary of State for Environment, Food and Rural Affairs, issued a statement to parliament about bTB and badgers, which declared that government policy was that licences would not be issued to allow badger culling to control bTB for fear that the cull might make things worse. He went on to say that £20 million would be invested in vaccinations for badgers and cattle over three years. Mr Benn also intimated that he wanted to work closely with the industry in order to find the appropriate solution and, in conjunction with Defra, a Bovine TB Partnership Group was to be established. After the success of its work, in 2012, Jim Paice the Agriculture Minister announced a new Bovine TB Eradication Advisory Group for England which was to broaden into areas of conservation.

While Defra statistics show a notable decrease in the incidence rate in 2012 in cattle (mainly as a result of an increased number of tests on unrestricted herds), last year 26,000 cattle were still slaughtered. The incidence rate is 4.2%, compared with 6.0% in June 2011. Defra, however, advises that this figure should not be accepted as 100% accurate, as it includes a number of unclassified incidents and there will be further revisions made. Herd incidents during the period January to June 2012 was 2,706, compared with 2,720 for January to June 2011. The number of tests on officially bTB-free herds was 41,656 in January to June 2012, compared with 34,667 in January to June 2011. The number of cattle compulsorily slaughtered as reactors or direct contacts was 18,213 in January to June 2012, compared with 18,081 in January to June 2011.

That said, there is a growing debate at the moment as there is huge resistance to the culling of badgers; opponents say that it risks increasing the spread of bTB instead of decreasing it. Leading experts on animal diseases say that, even if the increase does not materialise, culling is very unlikely to eradicate the spread of bTB, and they are angered over government plans that suggest a cull of 70% of badgers in an area will stop the spread of bTB. Many high-profile figures have joined the opposition, with Queen guitarist Brian May publicly lending his support, and a petition to stop the cull has been signed and sent to parliament.

Bluetongue disease

Bluetongue, which has now been downgraded by Defra in its level of severity, is an insect-borne viral disease to which all species of ruminants are susceptible, although sheep are most severely affected. It is characterised by changes to the mucous linings of the mouth and nose and the coronary band of the foot. It was first described in South

Africa but has since been recognised in most countries in the tropics and sub-tropics. Since 1999, there have been widespread outbreaks in Greece, Italy, Corsica and the Balearic Islands. Cases have also occurred in Bulgaria, Croatia, Macedonia and Serbia. It appears that the virus has spread from both Turkey and north Africa. One possible reason for the changing pattern of bluetongue disease in the Mediterranean region is climate changes. In September 2007, the first suspected UK case was reported in a Highland cow in Ipswich, Suffolk. Since then the virus has spread from cattle to sheep in Britain.

The clinical signs can vary from unapparent to mild or severe, depending on the virus strain and the breed of sheep involved. Deaths of sheep in a flock can be as high as 70%. Animals that survive the disease will lose condition, with a reduction in meat and wool production.

Bluetongue has been found in Australia, the USA, Africa, the Middle East and other parts of Asia and in Europe – with cases reported in the Netherlands, Belgium, parts of western Germany and areas of northern France. In order to control the infection, a protection zone boundary of 20km is set up to control the movement of animals and a further surveillance zone of 150km is put in place to monitor for any signs of the disease spreading. In the restriction zone, rules apply to the movement of ruminants, export of animals is prohibited and all animals on premises within this zone have to be identified and checked for bluetongue.

After bluetongue serotype 6 (BTV6) was confirmed on three farms in the Netherlands, as a result, on 20 October 2008 all exports from the Netherlands to other EU member states were banned as a precautionary measure while these cases were investigated. The ban is still in place. Whilst there is no ban on exports from Great Britain, there are still bans on imports from certain European zones. There are no reports of transmission to humans. On 5 July 2011, Great Britain was declared bluetongue free.

Canine influenza

Canine influenza refers to a new strain of the influenza A virus that causes influenza in canines. It is a contagious respiratory disease that often has the same signs as kennel cough – sneezing, coughing and fever – and requires veterinary medical attention. The disease came to light at a Florida racetrack when greyhound fatalities from respiratory illnesses were attributed to a mutated strain of the deadly equine influenza virus (H3N8) that has been detected in horses for over 40 years. Dogs have no natural immunity to this virus owing to a lack of previous exposure and therefore transmission rates between canines are recorded as being very high. Having affected the majority of American states, this specific strain of the influenza virus has now reached endemic levels. Statistically, roughly 100% of canines that come into contact with the virus – regardless of age or vaccination history – become infected. Of those infected, 20% show no signs of the virus. Of the 80% that exhibit signs, there have been two forms observed:

- mild infection – symptoms include a low fever, possible nasal discharge and a persistent cough that can last for anything up to three weeks
- severe infection – symptoms include a high fever, increased respiratory rates, which lead to difficulty breathing, and potentially other indicators of pneumonia.

However, the more positive news is that research shows fatality in only 8% of infected canines, making it a disease with a high morbidity but a low mortality rate.

Canine influenza is believed to be a mainly airborne virus – i.e. it is transmitted by sneezing or coughing – with an affected dog able to spread the virus for seven to 10 days after contracting the strain. Symptoms will present within two to five days. It is also worth bearing in mind that infected dogs can spread the virus without exhibiting signs of disease in themselves.

Treatment of canine influenza will vary from case to case. Early symptoms may require only a course of antibiotics to stop any secondary bacterial infections, but more serious cases could require the same treatment that humans receive in influenza cases, i.e. fluids (supplied intravenously in severe cases) and rest. There is, as yet, no recognisable vaccine to prevent canine influenza, although investigation continues into a canary pox-vectored vaccine – used for the treatment of equine influenza – for use in dogs. The virus is not known to infect humans or poultry.

MRSA

Methicillin-resistant *Staphylococcus aureus* (MRSA) – or 'superbug' – is a major health concern for causing outbreaks in hospitals around the UK. Primarily affecting humans, as the BVA says, it may also colonise and cause infection in companion and farm animals. MRSA is of little risk to healthy animals and, although transmission of infection from animals to humans has been documented, the rate is thought to be low. The evidence available points to humans as the source of the MRSA strains.

Staphylococcus aureus is a bacterium, strains of which live harmlessly on the skin and in the nose of about a third of normal healthy people. The problem arises when it enters the body, and it thrives in hospitals among those who are more susceptible due to the nature of their illnesses weakening their immune systems. MRSA can often enter the body through cuts, grazes and wounds, whether accidental or deliberate, i.e. those made out of necessity for surgery.

Different strains of MRSA usually affect animals and humans. They are particularly adept at colonising and/or infecting their preferred host species. For example, the staphylococci that commonly infect and colonise dogs are usually from a different species, known as *Staphylococcus intermedius*, which differs in certain characteristics from *Staphylococcus aureus*. Although strains of the latter may have a preferred host species, they can opportunistically infect other species in some circumstances.

Reported cases of MRSA infection in animals can be traced back to 1999 and are often reported in the media, although there was an incident back in the mid-1980s regarding a cat that lived in a rehabilitation ward for the elderly. Since then, dogs, cats, rabbits and horses have all been diagnosed with the MRSA infection. This problem is not isolated to the UK, but is seen throughout the world, with cases reported in the USA, Korea, Japan and Brazil. There is evidence of pigs now being affected in the Netherlands.

Most MRSA infections, particularly in cats and dogs, have been postoperative infections, usually from wounds, though the numbers of skin, ear, urinary tract and bronchial infections have been lower recently. There is evidence of a new strain affecting pigs and poultry but there is still no link with the human virus strain.

MRSA is a problem that will continue to trouble both humans and animals, because the effectiveness of antibiotics is constantly being challenged by the virus developing resistance to the drug.

Foot-and-mouth disease

The outbreak of foot-and-mouth disease (FMD) that occurred in February 2001 was the first in the UK for 20 years. Between February and September, 2,030 cases occurred. The last major outbreak was in 1967, during which about half a million animals were slaughtered. Before the re-emergence of the disease, in a new and highly virulent form, it had been thought that FMD had been eradicated from western Europe. The latest form of the virus seems to have originated in Asia, and could have been brought into the UK in a number of ways. Something as trivial as a discarded sandwich containing meat from an infected source – brought into the country by, for example, a tourist – could have been incorporated into pigswill (pig feed made from waste food) and then passed on to animals from other farms at a livestock sale. The bovine spongiform encephalopathy (BSE) problem (see page 79) led to greater regulation of abattoirs, which resulted in the closure of many smaller abattoirs. Animals destined for slaughter now have to travel greater distances and the possibility of FMD being passed to other animals is, as a consequence, greater.

The UK was declared FMD-free on 14 January 2002, almost a year after the first reported case. More than 4 million animals, from over

7,000 farms, were slaughtered during this period. The last recorded case occurred at the end of September 2001. The official report into the outbreak highlighted the lack of speed with which the government acted and commented on the fact that the understaffed State Veterinary Service (now called Animal Health) was unable to effectively monitor the disease. The disease took a month to diagnose and, by the time animal movement was halted, over 20,000 infected sheep had spread the virus across the UK.

Defra states that:

> 'FMD is endemic in parts of Asia, Africa and South America, with sporadic outbreaks in disease-free areas. Countries affected by FMD include Afghanistan, Bhutan, Iran, Lebanon, Peru, South Africa, the United Arab Emirates and Vietnam.'
>
> www.defra.gov.uk

There have been no outbreaks of the disease in the EU since the 2001 outbreak, which affected not only the UK but also Ireland, France and the Netherlands. A Royal Society report recommended that vaccination – commonly used in a number of countries – should be a weapon in any future outbreaks. Vaccination is unpopular with some meat exporters since it is difficult to distinguish between animals that have been vaccinated and those that have the disease, and for this reason many FMD-free countries ban the import of vaccinated cattle.

FMD is a viral disease that affects cattle, pigs, sheep, goats and deer. Hedgehogs and rats (and elephants!) can also become infected, and people, cats, dogs and game animals can carry infected material. The virus can be transferred by saliva, milk and dung; it can also become airborne and travel large distances, perhaps as far as 150 miles. A vehicle that has driven through dung from an infected animal can carry the virus to other farms on its tyres. FMD is more contagious than any other animal disease, and the mortality rate among young animals is high.

The role of the veterinary surgeon in a suspected outbreak of FMD is not a pleasant one. If the existence of the disease is confirmed, the vet must make arrangements with Defra to ensure that all animals on the farm (and possibly on neighbouring farms) are slaughtered and then incinerated. For economic reasons, there is no question of the vet being allowed to try to treat infected animals.

There has been only one recorded case of FMD in a human being in Great Britain and that was in 1966. The general effects of the disease in that case were similar to influenza, with some blisters. It is a mild, short-lived, self-limiting disease. The Food Standards Agency has advised that the disease in animals has no implications for the human food chain.

Bovine spongiform encephalopathy (BSE)

BSE – commonly referred to as mad cow disease – was first identified in 1986, although it is possible that it had been known about since 1983. It is a neurological disease that affects the brains of cattle, and is similar to scrapie, a disease of sheep that has been known since the eighteenth century. In 1988, the government's working party, chaired by Sir Richard Southwood, stated that there was minimal risk to humans since, as scrapie was known not to spread to humans, neither would BSE. It is believed that BSE originated in cattle as a result of the practice of using the remains of diseased sheep as part of high-protein cattle feed in an attempt to increase milk yields. In 1989, the government recommended that specific offal – such as the brain and the spleen – should be discarded rather than allowed to enter the food chain, and that diseased cattle should be incinerated. In the early 1990s, the increased incidence of Creutzfeldt–Jakob disease (CJD) – a disease similar to BSE that affects humans – caused scientists to look at the possibility that the disease had jumped species. At about the same time, scientists found increasing evidence of transmission between species following experiments involving mice, pigs and cats. By 1993, there were over 800 new cases of BSE a week, despite the ban on animal feed containing specified offal. It became clear that the increase in the cases of CJD was related to the rise in BSE, and that it was likely that millions of infected cattle had been eaten before the symptoms appeared. In 1996, the EU banned the export of cattle, beef and beef products that originated in the UK. In 1997, the government set up a public inquiry, chaired by Lord Phillips. The findings were released in October 2000 and details can be found on the inquiry website (http://collections.europarchive.org/tna/20090505194948/http:/bseinquiry.gov.uk/report/index.htm). The total number of confirmed cases of BSE in Great Britain since 1986 is estimated to be about 185,000. There has been an overall decline in the epidemic in recent years, with confirmed cases now falling by around 50%–100% each year since 2006.

The BSE problem raised a number of issues concerning farming and food safety. In retrospect, the decision to allow the remains of diseased animals to be incorporated into feed for herbivores seems to be misguided, at the very least. The problem with BSE is that the infecting agent, the prion (a previously unknown pathogen composed of proteins), was able to survive the treatments used to destroy bacteria and viruses. If any good has come out of the problem, it is that we are now much more aware of food safety. In April 2000, the government established the Food Standards Agency, created to 'protect public health from risks which may arise in connection with the consumption of food, and otherwise to protect the interests of consumers in relation to food'. Although it was established by the government, it can independently publish any advice that it gives the government, in order to avoid the accusations of cover-ups and secrecy levelled at the government over the BSE affair.

In March 2006, EU veterinary experts agreed unanimously to lift the ban on British beef exports, imposed 10 years earlier to prevent the spread of BSE. The EU's standing committee on the food chain and animal health said that the UK had fulfilled all the conditions for the ban to end. The closure of export markets had cost the British beef industry around £675 million.

Animal obesity

Researchers at the University of Glasgow have found that six out of 10 pet dogs are overweight or obese and independent research has shown that one in three household pets are overweight. Like humans, animals are putting on weight as a result of a number of factors, including being fed scraps from the dinner table, lack of exercise and even how old or rich their owners are.

According to the university's website:

> 'The study in the Journal of Small Animal Practice *assessed the body condition of 696 dogs. Owners were asked how often they fed their dog, what type of food was given, how often the dog was exercised, and the owner's age and household income. The results showed that 35.3% of the dogs had an ideal body shape, 39% were overweight, and 20.4% were obese; a further 5.3% were underweight.'*
>
> Source: www.gla.ac.uk/news/archiveofnews/
> 2010/july/headline_164795_en.html

Obesity can have a huge impact on an animal's health as it exacerbates a range of medical conditions, including arthritis and expiratory airway dysfunction, as well as lifespan.

The income of the owners was a factor:

> 'The dogs whose owners earned less than £10,000 a year were much more likely to be obese or overweight than those whose owners earned £40,000 or more.'
>
> Source: www.gla.ac.uk/news/archiveofnews/
> 2010/july/headline_164795_en.html

Canine lungworm

Angiostrongylus vasorum (or French heartworm) is a parasitic condition that is usually found in canines. Typically found in the heart and major blood vessels, lungworm causes many problems for the dog. If left untreated, it can cause fatal damage. Younger dogs are far more likely to be affected.

The parasite is most often carried in slugs and snails and normally ingested by dogs eating these pests. Foxes are also to blame for spreading the disease around the country.

For anyone concerned about this, the signs to look out for are breathing difficulties, poor blood clotting, general sickness and changes in behaviour. Whilst the main concern is obviously for the animal, as untreated it can be fatal, the spread of infection is a major issue. Canine lungworm is spread between canines through larvae in the faeces rather than directly, and so the worry is that dogs will become infected through close contact with the faeces of other dogs. Unlike roundworm, humans cannot become infected with this.

While this particular lungworm is the major cause for concern at the moment, there are also other types that can affect dogs. See www.lungworm.co.uk for more information.

High Profile Breed (HPB) List for dogs

The Kennel Club is an organisation that advises on issues such as buying and breeding dogs and how best to keep them at home. It also acts as a lobbying committee for issues within the dog world if it believes that tougher action is required to prevent actions that put dogs at risk. In recent years, the European Convention Study Group/2002, set up by the Kennel Club, has identified a number of 'high-profile' breeds of dog, which they define as:

> 'A breed from time to time designated by the General Committee as requiring particular monitoring by reason of visible condition(s) which may cause health or welfare concerns.'

These breeds are usually added because someone, whether that be a member of the general public or a professional, has expressed concerns about the health or welfare of the animal. Once the concerns have been identified, the Kennel Club looks closely at the key issues to be addressed within the breed and at health surveys and reviews of the animal, and gets expert opinions on the animal's welfare. The Kennel Club then advises breed clubs on those issues and provides guidance on effective steps to be taken.

At the moment, the current dogs identified in the HPB List are:

- basset hound
- bloodhound
- bulldog
- chow chow
- Clumber spaniel
- dogue de Bordeaux
- French bulldog
- German shepherd dog

- mastiff
- Neapolitan mastiff
- Pekingese
- pug
- St Bernard
- shar pei.

NB The Chinese crested has been removed.

In order to remove a dog from the HPB List, ahead of the establishment of a new Dog Health Group Breed Standards and Conformation Sub-group (due 2013), breeders should submit a proposal for their breed to be removed from the list. The committee looks at the recent health survey of the breed, a report from a veterinary surgeon, supporting material from breed clubs, championship show judges' reports and quantitative data with specific veterinary comment. A formal re-evaluation takes place three years after removal.

Schmallenberg virus

The Schmallenberg virus is a disease spreading throughout the UK affecting livestock. As the virus has now spread to the north of England, Scotland has been put on high alert. The virus is thought to have travelled into the UK from infected midges over the Channel. It is not believed that the outbreak has been brought into the country through imported livestock. The European Centre for Disease Prevention and Control suggests that there is a low risk to public health. It is currently found in Belgium, Germany, the Netherlands and the UK.

Most commonly transmitted by midges, mosquitoes and ticks, it causes mild to moderate disease (milk drop, pyrexia and diarrhoea) in adult cattle and late abortion or birth defects in new-born cattle, sheep and goats.

Lower temperatures reduce the activity of the carriers and therefore the spread of the virus should slow down over the winter.

See www.defra.gov.uk/animal-diseases/a-z/schmallenberg-virus for more information.

Swine influenza virus

This is a very common occurrence in pig populations: about half of the USA's pigs are thought to have the virus. While the recent swine flu outbreak has made the news in terms of its effects on humans, transmission of the virus from pigs to humans is relatively uncommon and does not always lead to human influenza, often resulting only in the production of antibodies in the blood. While it is uncommon, people with regular exposure to pigs are at increased risk of swine flu infection. If this causes human influenza, it is called zoonotic swine flu.

In pigs, three influenza A virus subtypes (H1N1, H1N2 and H3N2) are the most common strains worldwide. In the United States, the H1N1 subtype was the major strain pre-1998; after this time, H3N2 subtypes have been isolated from swine. As of 2004, H3N2 virus in pigs and turkeys contained human (HA, NA and PB1), swine (NS, NP and M), and avian (PB2 and PA) genes.

Transmission of the influenza virus is between infected and unaffected animals, with close transport, intensive farming and airborne infection all reasons for the spread of infection. Wild boar are considered to spread the disease between farms. The symptoms are sneezing, coughing, lethargy, decreased appetite and difficulty breathing.

As swine influenza is rarely fatal to pigs, little effort is made to treat the infection, with efforts instead being focused on stopping the spread of infection between farms. Antibiotics do exist, though, and are used to treat the symptoms of influenza.

Intensive farming

Meat and dairy products feature prominently in the British diet. Although carbohydrates (such as pasta and rice) comprise a greater proportion of our diet than they did 10 years ago, we still eat protein in higher quantities than is consumed by our southern European neighbours. We also demand cheap food. The meat, poultry, dairy and egg industries are faced with a choice – to use technological methods in order to keep the price of their products as low as possible, or to allow the animals that they farm to lead more 'natural' lives, which would necessarily reduce yields and increase costs. The use of drugs, hormones and chemicals is almost universal in farming (except in the organic farming movement), as are methods to control the movement of livestock by the use of pens, cages or stalls.

The veterinary profession is faced with a number of difficult decisions. It has to balance the pressure to produce cheap food with its primary aim of maintaining and improving animal welfare. An example of this is the use of antibiotics. Antibiotics are used in farming to treat sick animals. However, they are also used to protect healthy animals against the diseases associated with intensive farming and as growth promoters. The Soil Association reports that about 1,225 tonnes of antibiotics are used each year in the UK, over 60% of which are used for farm animals or by vets. The problem with antibiotics is that bacteria become resistant to them, and overuse of antibiotics in animals has these serious effects:

- resistant strains of bacteria, such as salmonella and *Escherichia coli*, can be passed on to humans, causing illness and, in extreme cases, death

- bacteria can develop resistance to the drugs that are used to treat serious illness in humans.

Other issues that concern the veterinary profession include:

- the welfare of live farm animals that are exported for slaughter
- battery farming of poultry
- the use of growth hormones
- humane killing of farm animals in abattoirs.

The Protection of Animals Act 1911 contains the general law relating to the suffering of animals, and agricultural livestock is also protected by more recent legislation. New regulations incorporating EU law came into force in August 2000. The regulations cover laying hens, poultry, calves, cattle, pigs and rabbits. More specifically, the EU banned the use of veal crates from 2007 and traditional battery cages from 2012. Details of the regulations can be found on the Defra website (www.defra.gov.uk).

Fox hunting

While not necessarily an issue concerning vets, it is certainly something that you should have an appreciation of as it does concern the animal world. Most people have a view on the issue of hunting with hounds. Prior to the Hunting Act of 2004, there were those, on the one hand, who argued that fox hunting was an integral part of rural life and a countryside tradition, that foxes kill farm animals and therefore need to be controlled, that thousands of rural jobs would be lost if it were banned, and that a ban on fox hunting would lead to a ban on other pastimes, such as shooting and fishing. On the other hand, many people believed that it was a cruel and unnecessary way to control foxes, claiming that around 20,000 foxes were killed every year and that about half that number of hunting dogs were also killed taking part in the sport. Animal rights activists believed it was immoral to chase and kill animals for sport.

The Hunting Act 2004, which banned fox hunting in England and Wales, took effect in February 2005. The Act makes it an offence to hunt a wild mammal with a dog. Nevertheless, some forms of hunting are exempt, including those using no more than two dogs to flush out a mammal to be shot. Controversy on what is a very emotive subject therefore still remains. On the first anniversary of the ban, in February 2006, hunt supporters called for the Act to be repealed while the League Against Cruel Sports accused 33 hunts of repeatedly breaching the law.

For opposing sides of an argument which continues to be pursued, you should investigate the websites hosted by the League Against Cruel Sports (www.league.uk.com) and the Countryside Alliance (www.countryside-alliance.org).

Fall in dairy prices

The UK is the ninth largest milk producer in the world and the third largest in Europe. Although largely (90%) self-sufficient in milk, the UK participates in a significant trade in milk production. Nevertheless, farmers' unions are warning that the UK dairy industry is facing meltdown unless a national dairy body is established that can regulate farm-gate milk prices.

Milk prices have been low for a number of years and this has been reflected in dairy farm incomes. Prices are expected to fall further as a result of the reform of the Common Agricultural Policy (CAP). Of additional concern to farmers is the fact that some sectors of the supply chain, for example supermarkets, are earning far greater profits than others. As a consequence, some dairy farmers are leaving the industry.

The Dairy Supply Chain Forum is working hard to understand why these farmers are leaving. While it is likely that profitability is an important factor, there are also issues such as succession of ownership and possibilities for diversification that need to be considered. In an open letter to the prime minister, in September 2006, one farm business consultant, David Hughes, referred to the plight of UK dairy farmers as follows.

> 'Today UK milk producers receive approximately 10 pence per pint for milk that costs 11.5 pence per pint to produce. The same milk retails for at least 27 pence per pint in the major supermarkets or up to 48 pence per pint on the doorstep. Production costs have been pared to the bone and there is little or nothing that family farms can do to achieve further savings. Put simply, the balance of power within the supply chain is weighted entirely in favour of the large retailers, with a relatively weak processing sector competing to meet their demands. The individual milk producer has no bargaining power at all. If society chooses to ignore this gross imbalance of power we will rapidly witness the demise of the family-run dairy farm. They will be replaced by a small number of industrial milk factories that will contribute nothing to our countryside. Worse still, we could end up importing our entire milk supply with all the attendant strategic risks and environmental damage caused by increased food miles.'

In 2012 this remains as much of an issue as ever, and in July 2012 about 2,000 famers gathered in London to protest about cuts of up to 2p a litre of the overall total they would receive for the milk they sold. In an interview with the BBC, Agriculture Minister Jim Paice gave the example that an average pint of milk costs 49p, of which the dairy farmer receives only 16p, which is putting a 'massive burden' on them.

Dangerous Dogs Act

The Dangerous Dogs Act, which was introduced in 1991, banned the ownership, breeding, sale and exchange and advertising for sale of specified types of fighting dogs. The dogs covered by the ban included the pit bull terrier. The Act was amended in 1997, one of the effects of which was to lift the mandatory destruction orders that courts applied to dogs found to be of those types listed in the Act. It is now possible, therefore, for prohibited dogs to be added to the Index of Exempted Dogs, but only at the direction of a court and only if the necessary conditions are met (tattooing, microchipping, etc.). No owner may apply to have their dog added to the index – it is entirely a matter for the courts to decide upon. The maximum penalty for illegal possession of a prohibited dog is a fine of £5,000 and/or six months' imprisonment.

Should this issue arise at interview, it is important to demonstrate that you are aware that vicious attacks by certain breeds of unmuzzled dogs on children and adults led to the Act requiring owners to register such dogs with the police and to keep them muzzled. For the qualified vet, controversy might arise if they are called on to destroy, for example, an unmuzzled pit bull terrier before it has committed an offence.

Is such action contrary to the professional oath of a veterinary surgeon? (Privately, many vets say that the Act is unworkable.) If you take a view on this in an interview you will get credit for at least knowing about the law, whether the interviewer agrees with your conclusion or not.

Hybrid dogs

In a consumer-focused society, designer dogs have become the new fad. But does this pose any danger? From labradoodles to puggles, dogs are turning into handbag accessories rather than family pets or functional animals. Originally these designer dogs were designed as a hypo-allergenic version of the guide dog, but the issue of hybrid breeds throws up an ethical question. Hybrid dogs are now sold for staggering amounts of money, and it does ask questions of what hope is there for the adoption of other dogs and for rescue shelters. However, the advantage of breeding designer or hybrid dogs can often be a reduction in the level of genetic defects or health problems found in particular breeds of pedigree dog. The hybrid dog has a much larger genetic pool and therefore a lower risk of suffering from the same health problems of either one of its parents. Hybrid dog breeding remains a controversial topic but one that you should know about and be happy to comment on in terms of both advantages and disadvantages.

Animal testing

Almost all of the drugs used to treat people have been tested on animals. Without rigorous and controlled testing there are significant health risks associated with the use of new medicines. In many cases, the long-term or side effects of drugs can be more serious than the illness itself, and testing is therefore essential. Lord Winston, who pioneered in vitro fertilisation (IVF) and who found wider publicity through his BBC television series *The Human Body*, in response to a report by the House of Lords Select Committee on Science and Technology, was quoted in the *Independent* as saying: 'Perceived pressure may persuade people to go down a route which is not going to promote human welfare. We have a major job – animal research is essential for human welfare. Every drug we use is based on it. Without it those drugs would be unsafe.'

Each year British laboratories experiment on approximately 3 million animals. British law requires that any new drug must be tested on at least two different species of live mammal, one of which must be a large non-rodent. UK regulations are considered some of the most rigorous in the world – the Animals (Scientific Procedures) Act 1986 insists that no animal experiments be conducted if there is a realistic alternative.

The debate on animal testing has become a high-profile one because of the activities of animal rights groups. Although the majority of animal rights groups campaign peacefully, the newspapers have given a good deal of publicity to a number of attacks on research laboratories. Huntingdon Life Sciences (HLS), a 60-year-old product development company, has been at the forefront of recent controversy over animal testing. The company claims that it works with a variety of resources, including pharmaceuticals and veterinary products, to help its manufacturers develop safer goods for the market. Some of its opponents claim that HLS kills 500 animals a day in tests for products such as weed killer, food colourings and drugs.

In April 2003, HLS won a High Court injunction preventing protesters going within 50 yards of the homes of staff. In the same month, activists held protests at three colleges of Cambridge University against the proposal for a primate experimentation laboratory at Girton College. Oxford University, like HLS, sought to obtain an injunction against animal rights protesters following opposition to a new research laboratory. Like HLS, Oxford was also successful. Protests and demonstrations, however, concerning these cases and other cases of animal testing continue to this day.

Opposition to animal testing is centred on the idea that if animals are similar enough to us for test results to be meaningful, then they are too similar to be experimented upon. Conversely, drugs tested on animals have also gone on to have devastating effects on humans. Examples are the drug thalidomide and the drug trial in March 2006 that caused six men to have multiple organ failure. Campaigners argue that there are alternative methods of testing that do not involve animals. Many of these methods are, they say, also cheaper, quicker and more effective. They include:

- culture of human cells – this is already used in research into cancer, Parkinson's disease and acquired immune deficiency syndrome (AIDS)
- molecular methods, including DNA analysis
- use of micro-organisms
- computer modelling
- use of human volunteers.

Other issues

In addition to the topics listed above, it is advisable for an aspiring vet to have some prior knowledge of other issues that have affected the profession over the past decade. You are also strongly advised to check out the Defra website and look at some of the other global issues affecting animals today, such as African horse sickness, koi herpes virus and West Nile virus.

Case study

Are you ever truly prepared for the realities of such a demanding job? This is a very difficult question to answer. Kim qualified from Edinburgh six years ago and is currently working in general practice. 'You can never underestimate the importance of sound theory and training, but more than that, you can never underestimate the value of experience. I got first-rate training from Edinburgh – the balance between scientific and medical aspects of the course was just right, and the emphasis on the practical side of the profession was invaluable. As a result of the hard work undertaken on the course, I had confidence on graduating that I could handle any likely situation. It is amazing how much more there is to learn upon leaving university, though. It was almost as though the course had merely scratched the surface. This, of course, is not the case, but it is true to say that only by putting the theory into practice can an aspiring vet appreciate what it is like to be a vet.

'It is a job with incredible diversity, and indeed diversity that can change on a knife edge. With all the changes in the industry and the current economic and political climate, which does have an

effect on the veterinary world as well, it is of the utmost importance that any professional keeps themselves well informed. This
can be hard as a vet's hours are long and arduous – but keep your
ear to the ground. It is known as continuing professional development (CPD) and it is a requirement of the RCVS. It might seem
like the last thing you wish to do after a long week, but CPD
allows vets to network with others in the profession through
training sessions where we can discuss the updated trends.'

Like many other vets we have heard from, Kim's interest in
veterinary science started when she was very young, when she
used to go riding with a friend back home in Birmingham. Unlike
many others, though, Kim was accepted to veterinary school as
a graduate, only arriving at the decision to work in the veterinary
profession after first studying for a degree in biology. Having
made this decision late, Kim had to take any opportunity in order
to gain the relevant work experience, so she appreciates the
value of hard work and likes those who undertake work experience with her to display that same drive. Now Kim is working as
a veterinary surgeon and hopes to own her own practice in the
not-too-distant future.

8 | A leopard does not change its spots
Non-standard applicants

This book has focused on those students who are applying on a 'standard' application with A levels. However, those are not the only qualifications that will be considered. There are a large number of overseas applicants applying for veterinary medicine each year and this is discussed in this chapter, alongside those wishing to study overseas, mature students and also those with special needs.

Overseas students

The competition for places at veterinary school is high and it would be sensible to email an admissions tutor to discuss your application informally with the university before submitting it. If you have not taken A levels or the International Baccalaureate (IB), this does not mean that you will not get a place. However, you do need to have a qualification recognised by English institutions and you need to refer directly to the universities with your specific qualification for advice. Information about qualifications can also be obtained from British Council offices in your country (www.britishcouncil.org). The UCAS website also has a section for international students which describes in detail the applications process and deadlines.

BMAT

At certain veterinary universities, there is no requirement for overseas applicants to sit the BMAT examination. The RVC, for instance, does not require overseas applicants to sit it; home and EU students are required to take the test only because the volume of applicants is so high and so it is an extra filter. Taking the test will not be seen as giving you an advantage over other international students.

Fees

Overseas students are liable for the full cost of tuition. Universities do have international scholarships available. For these you apply directly to the university. See Chapter 10 for more information on fees and funding.

English language qualifications

In order to prove your English ability you must pass an English language test. The most common tests are the IELTS (International English Language Testing System) and TOEFL (Test of English as a Foreign Language). You should be looking at achieving at least IELTS 6.5 to 7.0 in order to begin the university course and certainly no less than 6.5 in each band. In the TOEFL, anything from 93 or above will be required. Most universities will set this boundary higher in order to discourage some applications.

Visas

International students will have to apply for a Tier 4 Student Visa before they are able to study in the UK. In order to get a Tier 4 Student Visa you will need a CAS (Confirmation of Acceptance for Studies) from the individual university where the offer was given. In order to get a CAS, you will need to show various documents as set out by the admissions department. This can take time – there is no way of saying how much time as that will vary from country to country, but it can be days or weeks. The important thing is for you to apply for a CAS as soon as you are able.

Studying outside the UK

An option open to students who wish to study overseas, but want to undertake some of their clinical training in one of the UK veterinary schools, is the veterinary science course offered by St George's University in Grenada, West Indies. Another place that may be of interest is the Faculty of Medicine at Kosice, Slovak Republic, where the course is taught in English and accredited by the RCVS. For contact details for the course, see Chapter 12.

It is possible to practise as a vet in the UK having studied overseas. The process is simpler for students who have studied in the EU, or in certain universities in Canada, Australia, South Africa or New Zealand where their degrees are approved by the RCVS. Those with European degrees can also register with the RCVS if they have EU community rights entitlement (entitlement rights to work in a member state). Details are listed on the RCVS website.

However, graduates from other countries can still practise in the UK if they pass the statutory examination for membership of the RCVS, which is held in a UK veterinary school in May/June each year. Further information for all overseas graduates can be obtained from the RCVS website (www.rcvs.org.uk).

Mature students

In view of the extreme competition for places, it is unrealistic for mature students, at, say, 25 or 30 years of age, to expect special treatment. They should expect to satisfy the academic entry requirements in the usual way at one recent sitting and must have a good range of practical experience. However, this requirement has been known to be waived in exceptional cases, such as where a mature student displays strong motivation coupled with academic ability.

Mature applicants should use the personal statement section of the UCAS application to set out their qualifications and work experience. Your objective is to signal to the admissions tutors why they should see you. Your extra maturity and practical experience should show here. If you cannot get all the information in the space allowed, make sure you summarise what you want to get across in accordance with the bullet points in Chapter 6 (see page 53) – why you want to study veterinary science, what you have done to explore this decision, how you respond to people, how you react under pressure, what your career aspirations are, and what your extracurricular interests are in order to show that you are a rounded individual.

Remember, it is very important to show why you want to work with animals and to give details of any relevant work experience of a paid or voluntary nature. If you feel that the space in the personal statement section of the UCAS application does not permit you to do full justice to yourself, it is a good idea to prepare a CV or further documentation and send this directly to the veterinary school with your UCAS application number.

Students with disabilities and special educational needs

Students with disabilities and special educational needs are welcome at all institutions and are not disadvantaged. If you have a disability or health condition, you are encouraged to look at the demands of the course at the individual university. Those with a hearing or visual impairment are equally encouraged to apply. The institutions are fully committed to support students with needs, from dyslexia to physical disability, and have access arrangements in place. It is advisable in each situation to contact the universities individually and explain to them your circumstances as well as including details on the UCAS form. The more information you can give them, the better they will be able to advise you on what arrangements are in place. Provisions are usually made within the teaching facilities, though some forms of accommodation may pose more of a logistical problem.

In terms of special educational needs, students who require a word processor or extra time will be allowed these in the same way that they would have been at school, subject to providing the correct documentation to the university.

For more information, refer directly to the university, which will probably have a person in charge of special access arrangements.

9 | A bird in the hand
Results day

It is 16 August – the dreaded results day. No matter how much preparation went in, there will always be nerves on the day. The best case scenario is, of course, that you meet the grade requirements for your offer. In that situation you can check your UCAS Track and see that your offer has been made unconditional. The next step is for the university to contact you directly. However, you need to be prepared for other scenarios in case the results do not match your predictions.

What to do if you hold no offer

There are a number of students who will approach results day without having received an offer from a veterinary school. In the past, if you found yourself in this position and secured excellent grades in your A levels, it may have been possible to find a place through Clearing. Unfortunately, it is now virtually impossible for a student to secure a place on a veterinary course in this way, even if they hold outstanding grades. This situation is unlikely to change in coming years. Ultimately, though, Clearing may be of use to secure a place on an alternative course.

If you hold three A or A* grades but were rejected when you applied through UCAS (i.e. you did not get an offer), you need to let the veterinary schools know that you are out there, and discuss options for how you may secure a place in the future. The best way to do this is by phone or email directly. They will be busy on results day so bear with the institutions around that time. There is no substitute to establishing a good rapport with an admissions tutor – they will be able to give you guidance on exactly what you need to do next and what they are looking at.

The most likely scenario is that you will have to reapply through UCAS in the next admissions cycle. Although you will already have the grades for entry in this situation, it is important to understand that there are a number of other elements of your application that you'll need to work on to maximise your chances of securing a place. Things to consider are listed below.

- Your personal statement – revisit it and cast a critical eye over it. This is also an opportunity to add in any work placements or other positive experiences that you have had since your last application.

- Your BMAT score – you will need to resit your BMAT for each admissions cycle. This will give you a chance to complete further practice questions and learn from your experience of sitting it first time around. It may also be a good idea to attend one of the BMAT preparation courses that are available.
- Your work experience – any opportunity to add further work experience to your profile will always be a good step. Whether it is veterinary-related or just general voluntary work, it will have a positive impact. That said, focus on applying for veterinary places as much as you can as this is what will show you are still focused on this course despite the setback.

What to do if you have good grades but no offer

There is a system called UCAS Adjustment that allows applicants who pass their exams with better results than expected to get a place at a higher-level university. However, this is not likely to be the case for veterinary school as they all require high grades and you would not have been made an offer that required lower grades. You can enter Adjustment only if your results have met and exceeded the conditions of your conditional firm choice. A student must have held a conditional firm choice on their application to be eligible, and so, if you have had no offers, it is not something you can use. In short, Adjustment doesn't help if you have applied to veterinary schools.

What to do if you hold an offer but miss the grades

If you have only narrowly missed the required grades, it is important that you contact the admissions team as soon as possible. As mentioned previously, you will probably know what their decision is at this point, thanks to the UCAS website. If you have been rejected, it is vital that you keep a level head and do not panic; you must stay calm throughout. If you have not been rejected outright or are unsure of their decision, you must contact the admissions team by telephone – so ensure that in the run-up to results day you have gathered together the contact numbers of the universities you have accepted as your firm and insurance choices.

In some cases, veterinary schools will allow applicants who hold a conditional offer to slip a grade (particularly if they came across well at the interview stage) rather than offering the place to somebody else. It will depend on how much you have missed the grade by – with uniform mark scale (UMS) points nowadays that is easy to ascertain. However, be warned – this is a rare occurrence and most of the time dropping a grade will result in outright rejection.

When speaking to the universities, they are likely to give you a simple yes or no answer or tell you that you are still being considered. It is unlikely that crying, begging or pleading your case to the person on the phone will make any difference to the overall decision. If they tell you that you have been rejected, there are some questions you should ask.

- Would they consider your application if you applied next year (i.e. do they accept resit students)?
- What would the likely grade requirements be? (They will almost certainly ask for at least AAA, but it is worth checking anyway.)
- Would they interview you again?

If at all possible, get something in writing for reference later on, towards the application time.

Retaking A levels

Many unsuccessful candidates decide to do a repeat year and take their examinations again. Before doing this it would be sensible to seek the advice of an admissions tutor. The fact is that not many people doing repeats are made conditional offers unless there are documented extenuating circumstances, such as serious illness. If you are made an offer it will usually be based upon the second attempt and the requirement will probably be raised to achieving grade A in all three subjects. You may get a repeat offer if you have narrowly failed to secure a place on the first try and are excellent in all other respects.

The truth is that the almost overwhelming pressure of demand by highly motivated and well-qualified candidates is taking its toll on the chances of those repeating A levels. Selection is becoming more stringent, resulting in fewer resitters being successful.

Retakes are considered by universities depending on the specific policy of the institution you are applying to. In most cases the policy is that students can retake without penalty; however, you must get the highest possible grade in the second sitting. There can also be the condition placed on you that you have to have achieved a minimum grade in a specific subject at AS level. Retakes within a two-year course are accepted without problem.

It is possible to improve A level grades by retaking anything between one and six units, depending on how many times the units have been sat and how close you are to the A grade boundary. It is often sensible to retake AS units as they are easier than the A2 units. To achieve an A grade at A level you need to score 480 UMS marks out of 600, and it does not matter how the 480 marks are achieved, so it makes sense to gain as many of the 'easier' marks as possible. Your retake strategy will depend on how many extra marks you need and which examination board set your papers (which will determine when resits are available). Sixth-form colleges are usually happy to advise students about their options.

Case study

Having narrowly missed out on his A level grades, 19-year-old Joshua is currently studying to resit two of his subjects in January. Despite seeing all his friends go to university, Joshua has not been deterred and, instead of seeing it as a setback, he has taken it as an opportunity.

Joshua is not concerned about the geographical locations of the veterinary schools, and so he has made his choices based on the universities' specific work experience requirements. His father is a doctor, as is his mother, so Joshua has grown up surrounded by medical language. However, while interested in the human physique, it was the diversity of the animal kingdom that drew Joshua's focus.

'I have always liked animals since I went to a petting zoo at the age of four, and in many ways, I think that I have always known that I wanted to be a vet. Despite currently living in London, I was lucky enough to grow up in the valleys of Wales where my father still works. On many occasions, I helped our local farmers with the sheep on the hills, feeding them, shearing them and also with the lambing. Knowing exactly what I wanted to do with my life, I applied for work experience in a variety of different places, both internationally and on the home front, and was even lucky enough to work at the RSPCA Harmsworth Memorial Hospital under the excellent tutelage of David Grant.

'I know that everyone claims this but I genuinely have always tried hard at my academic subjects even though I do not naturally find them easy. I did not apply last year and I am grateful that I did not as I narrowly missed the required grades. Aside from anything else though, I wanted to gain as much experience as possible. Resitting my exams has been the best possible way forward for me as I feel more grounded now, even three months on.'

Providing that you meet the requirements of the specific university – both academically and practically – you should not feel disadvantaged when applying. It is worth remembering that there remains a slight shortage of vets at the moment; however, that does not mean they take just anyone!

Reapplying

In order to reapply, you have to go through exactly the same process again, taking into account all that has been said above. However, when reapplying, make sure you update your application. A careless application would be one that does not include anything new about what you have planned – or worse, it does not update a personal statement to the present tense!

Make sure that you talk to admissions tutors about your chances before you reapply, as they may suggest that you take a three-year degree in a related subject, Bioveterinary Science for example, and then apply for graduate entry. It is important to take their opinion on board as they are the ones who will be making the decision.

If you had extenuating circumstances first time round, then mention them at this point but make sure they are compelling – not just 'I had a cold on the day!'

Often it is better to reapply once you have your resit grades, even though this might mean waiting another year.

10 | Counting sheep
Financing your course

Once you arrive in veterinary school, you will want at least to avoid the worry of getting too deeply into debt. Money is a problem for all students and those studying veterinary science will have additional expenses connected with their course, mainly travel expenses, clothing, books and equipment. Veterinary students are also limited in the opportunities they have to earn extra money during the holidays because they have to spend time doing EMR to gain the prescribed experience in veterinary practice as part of their training. Students believe that sixth-formers and others preparing to go to veterinary school should be forewarned about coping with the money side of being a veterinary student.

First-year expenditure for veterinary students is particularly high and can easily exceed £9,000 for those living away from home.

Fees

UK students

Universities are now allowed to charge UK and EU students up to £9,000 a year for tuition fees. Most of the higher-ranked universities will charge the maximum amount. The average course fee across all institutions will be £8,393. You should refer to the websites of the specific universities to find out what they intend to charge, and also to the UCAS website – use the course search facility.

If you are a student resident in England, you will pay up to £9,000 wherever you study in the UK.

If you are a student resident in Scotland, you will not pay any tuition fees if you study at a Scottish university. You will pay up to £9,000 if you study elsewhere in the UK.

If you are a student resident in Wales, you will pay up to £9,000 wherever you study in the UK; however, you will be able to receive a £3,465 loan from the Welsh government, and you will also be eligible for a grant up to the difference between the loan and the full fee.

If you are a student resident in Northern Ireland, you will pay up to £9,000 if you study in England, Wales or Scotland but you will pay only £3,465 if you study in Northern Ireland.

EU students

If you are an EU student, you will pay up to £9,000 if you study in England or Northern Ireland, but no fee if you study in Scotland. You will receive the same help as Welsh students (see above) if you are studying at a Welsh university.

International student fees

Students from outside the EU pay more in tuition fees than UK or EU students. The fees for non-EU international students do not have a set upper limit. The fees will depend on the course and the university. The fees at the RVC are £22,000 per year for pre-clinical and clinical training (based on figures provided by the RVC for 2012–13). However, the figure for Nottingham is £20,420.

Funding

Loans

A non-means-tested tuition fees loan is available for tuition fees up to £9,000. This will be paid by the Student Loans Company and will be added to your overall loan. Your repayments are deferred until after you have left university and have started earning £21,000 or more per year.

A maintenance loan (student loan) is different from a tuition fees loan. This is a variable means-tested loan designed to aid with living costs. The table below shows what you are entitled to borrow.

Table 3 Expected maintenance loan for 2012–13

Location	Maximum loan
London	£7,675
Elsewhere	£5,500
Parental home	£4,375

Reprinted with kind permission of the RVC website (www.rvc.ac.uk)

Grants

A variable means-tested living cost grant (the maintenance grant) is available if your household income is up to £42,611. In this instance, you will be entitled to a grant of between £50 and £3,354, which you will need to pay back. (See www.gov.uk/student-finance/loans-and-grants for more information.)

Bursaries

The veterinary schools offer bursaries and further advice on sources of funding. You should read the websites of the universities in order to find out whether you will be able to get a reduction in fees. The RVC, for example, offers a means-tested bursary (see Table 4 below) and merit-based scholarships based on a number of indicators, including the interview and test scores.

Armed Forces bursaries are grants to selected veterinary students who pass their Army Officer Selection Board examinations and apply before their final university year. In return, you have to spend four years in the service. For more details, have a look online at www.army.mod.uk/join/20109.aspx.

National Scholarship Programme

If you are resident in England and your family's income is less than £25,000 per year, you will be eligible for help from the National Scholarship Programme (NSP). This can take the form of help with tuition fees, accommodation or other costs. The university will pay the scholarship and so the nature and size of the scholarship will vary from institution to institution. For more information, visit www.hefce.ac.uk/whatwedo/wp/currentworktowidenparticipation/nationalscholarshipprogramme/.

International students

There is no funding available for international students from universities so you must make sure you have the funding in place already. International bursaries are available (based on the admissions process where they consider academic strengths and means-tested conditions) to the value of one year's tuition fees. While you need to look at each university separately, have a look at the RVC website as an example of what is available (www.rvc.ac.uk/Undergraduate/Finances.cfm). Depending on where you are applying from, you should get in touch with the British Council in your country and find out what funding is available for you to study overseas. There is often funding available from a variety of sources within each country.

Students are able to apply for student loans by selecting option 02 (for local government authority) on the UCAS form under 'Fees and Funding'. You can also apply to the Student Loans Company for a loan. Find out more at www.slc.co.uk.

You should also visit the BVA website to find out more about sources of funding for veterinary students: www.bva.co.uk/public/documents/funding_sources.pdf.

Table 4 New entrants to veterinary medicine: maintenance support for 2012–13

Family income (£)	Assessed family contribution	Maintenance grant	RVC bursary	Grant/bursary total	Maintenance loan (max £6,928*)	Grant, loan and bursary total
25,000	0	2,906	1,650	4,556	5,475	10,031
30,000	0	1,906	1,082	2,988	5,975	8,963
34,400	0	1,106	628	1,734	6,375	8,109
39,333	0	755	429	1,184	6,551	7,735
40,000	0	711	0	711	6,573	7,284
45,000	0	381	0	381	6,738	7,119
50,020	0	50	0	50	6,903	6,953
50,778	0	0	0	0	6,928	6,928
55,000	844	0	0	0	6,084	6,084
60,000	1,844	0	0	0	5,084	5,084
60,478	1,940	0	0	0	4,988 (†)	4,988
65,000	1,940	0	0	0	4,988	4,988

Key

* Maximum loan calculated for a standard academic year. Courses at the RVC are often slightly longer and extra weeks' payments are added to this amount.

† This is the point at which the 72% non-means-tested element of the loan is recorded.

Reprinted with kind permission of the RVC website (www.rvc.ac.uk).

Keeping costs down: hints and tips

- Avoid buying lots of kit or textbooks in advance. When you get to the course you may find some discounts are offered. Second-hand textbooks may be for sale, although many veterinary students prefer to keep their textbooks for use in their working lives. Also try medical students for second-hand textbooks.
- Check for student travel concessions and get advice on the best offers on the regular trips that you will have to make.
- Apply early for the student loan, as it takes some time for the loan to be processed. Remind the bank about that overdraft facility they promoted to you when they sought your custom.
- Veterinary students work hard and like to play hard as well. Set yourself a limit on how much you are prepared to spend each term. Remember – the more partying, the worse your bank account will look. Perhaps you will go to the annual vet ball. If you do, why not consider buying the gear second-hand? By all means join the Association of Veterinary Students (AVS), but do you want to attend the congress or go on sports weekends? They all cost money.
- Easter is a time when it is possible for students to augment their income. Once you have gained experience with your first lambing, students say that it is possible, if you are lucky, to make over £300 per week. This is very hard work, involving 12 hours a day, for seven days a week, for a minimum of three weeks. But it will certainly improve your bank account – and give you valuable experience.

Expected student expenditure

The lists below, taken from the website of the Faculty of Biology, University of Cambridge (www.bio.cam.ac.uk/sbs/facbiol/mvst/Costs%20of%20studying.html), show the estimated additional course costs (2012/13) for students applying to veterinary science courses at that institution.

Vets

Overalls	£13.50
Lab coat	£8.50
Dissection kit, gloves, safety glasses, loan of locker and key, loan of dog skeleton	£24.00
Veterinary Dissection Manual which includes course guides for Veterinary Anatomy and Physiology (1st Year) and Neurobiology and Comparative Veterinary Biology (2nd Year)*	£14.00
Waterproof Trousers	£12.80

Wellington Boots (with toe-protector)	£12.00
University approved calculator	£14.00-£16.00
Electron micrographs (optional)	£ 2.00
EMS (preclinical) 12 weeks practical vacation experience with animals, particularly farm animals. Insurance cover provided but no subsistence grants payable	

* The manuals essentially replace the need for a textbook of human or veterinary anatomy.

Veterinary medicine (clinical)

Locker padlock	£2.35
Stethoscope	£4.95
Digital thermometer	£3.50
6" scissors curved on flat	£2.85
Spencer Wells Forceps 5"	£3.59
Pen Torch	£1.95
Dog lead (red)	£1.60
Hoof pick	£1.06

In addition to the list above, students will be required to purchase white theatre shoes and protective clothing to be worn in theatre, prior to starting their **6th year rotations**:

| White theatre shoes | £1.95 (approximate price) |
| Theatre scrubs | £12.20 (approximate price) |

Table 5, below, outlines the estimated expenditure for students for each pre-clinical year, living in London, at home and away from home.

Table 5 Expenditure estimate per pre-clinical year

Expenses	London (£)	Living away from home (£)	Living at home (£)
Tuition fees	Up to £9,000 per year	Up to £9,000 per year	Up to £9,000 per year
Overalls	£13.50	£13.50	£13.50
Lab coats	£8.50	£8.50	£8.50
Wellies	£12	£12	£12
Course notes	£75	£75	£75
Textbooks	£300	£300	£300
Travel costs	£600	£400	£400

EMS travel costs	£500	£350	£350
Student vet sub	£60	£60	£60
Social events	£1,200	£1,200	£1,200
Accommodation	£6,500	£4,000	N/A
Total	**£18,269**	**£15,419**	**£11,419**

No tuition fees are payable by Scottish students in Scotland. Non-UK European Union students studying in Scotland pay full international tuition fees.

Note: These figures, aside from the tuition fees which are applicable as of 2012–13 entry, were estimated in September 2012 and are intended only as a guide. Therefore, please refer to university websites for a detailed breakdown of the individual expenditure requirements.

Case study

Daniel is in the fourth year of his veterinary studies. He has opted to follow a six-year course which incorporates an intercalated BSc degree. His third year involved research projects in other departments of the university, and he gained a BSc in Anatomy. The reason that Daniel chose the intercalated BSc course is that his interests lie in the field of veterinary research rather than practice. He has a particular interest in equine medicine and behaviour, and chose his university because of its strong links with an equine hospital.

Daniel gained nine A grades at GCSE, and chose to study Biology, Chemistry, Physics and Psychology at A level. 'My interest was always in the theoretical side of practical work at school. I was always breaking things and my experiments would never work. It became a joke amongst my teachers and the others in my classes. When I told them that I wanted to study veterinary science at university, it caused great hilarity. My careers teacher gave me lots of help in preparing for my interviews, and we decided that the best option was to be very honest about my interest in research rather than try to pretend that I wanted to be a practising vet. Most of my work experience was in research. My school helped me to arrange some placements at Birmingham University during my A levels, working with postgraduates on molecular biology, and I was able to bring along reports to my interviews. I managed to get four A grades at A level, but it was a close-run thing because I didn't get high marks in my biology and chemistry coursework, and my physics practical exam was a disaster. The veterinary course is very practically focused and I have discovered that I enjoy this more than I thought I would. Not enough to make me want to change direction, though! My aim is to work in a university research department, and possibly in a pharmaceutical company later on.'

Most of Daniel's friends on the veterinary course want to work as veterinary surgeons. They particularly enjoy the practical side of the course, but can sometimes find the theoretical aspects difficult because they seem less relevant to the realities of working as a practising vet. 'Despite the different directions that we want to take in our careers,' says Daniel, 'we have one thing in common – we are all absolutely focused on our goals, and we work incredibly hard in order to achieve these. Studying veterinary science is demanding – I am sometimes jealous of friends studying arts subjects at the university because they have so much free time. They also have more money than I do because they all have part-time jobs – something I don't have time to do. However, they do not have clear ideas about where their lives are heading, which I do. I wouldn't swap places with them.'

11| Snakes and ladders
Career paths

There may be hidden expenses in training to be a vet, but at least you can reflect, with some optimism, that a degree in veterinary science is going to result in a professional qualification and a job. According to figures published in the RCVS's annual report for 2012, over 87.7% of registered surgeons were in practice and roughly 73% of those were in the UK (bear in mind that these figures only reflect those surgeons registered with the RCVS on 31 March 2012).

While in the past few years there has been cause for concern over a shortage of practising vets, the situation now is not as drastic as it has been. In 2011, veterinary surgeons were removed from the national jobs shortage list, which highlights areas of concern in terms of skilled jobs. That said there is a genuine concern that we have an impending shortage of vets with farm experience, which could leave the UK vulnerable to outbreaks of disease in livestock.

Professional Development Phase

Once you have graduated from your veterinary degree course, you are still not there yet. The year after graduation is known as the Professional Development Phase (PDP), during which you will be expected to develop your skills. The RCVS has developed a set of 'year one competencies' so that you can record your progress. After that you will always be expected to keep up with your CPD by attending courses and lectures and networking. Once you have qualified, you might wish to consider working in the types of practice or roles described in this chapter.

Career opportunities

The universities' first destination statistics show that nearly all veterinary graduates begin their careers in practice, but such is the variety of opportunity in this profession that career change and divergence can and does occur. Graduates are employed in the government service dealing with investigation, control and eradication of diseases. There are also opportunities for veterinary scientists to become engaged in university teaching and research establishments at home and abroad.

If you start in general practice, there is the chance to move into different types of practice. The trend is towards small-animal practices, but there is also more opportunity to work with horses – now seen as an important part of the growing leisure industry. There is also a growing trend towards specialisation within practices. Areas of specialisation include cattle, horses, household pets and even exotics. Specialisation can also be more sophisticated – for example, combining equine care with lameness in all animals. Dermatology, soft tissues and cardiology are examples of the kinds of specialisation that are seen as helpful to clients. It is possible for postgraduate specialist qualifications to be obtained through the RCVS's specialist certificate and diploma examinations.

Postgraduate courses

Education in the field of veterinary medicine is continuous. There are both full-time and part-time postgraduate courses, and they can focus on anything from the welfare of animals to infectious diseases to education. These programmes are designed for anyone looking to advance their knowledge of a specialist part of the profession through research. The postgraduate courses are not restricted to the seven veterinary schools but are available in a range of universities; you can take postgraduate courses in anything from Applied Animal Behaviour and Welfare at Newcastle University to Aquatic Veterinary Studies at the University of Stirling.

It is important to note that you do not need a postgraduate course in order to get employment in the profession. These courses are for those who wish to specialise or move into a niche field, such as aquatic veterinary medicine.

Veterinary variety: types of vet

As your degree progresses, you will most likely find an area of veterinary medicine that you particularly enjoy or have a certain flair for. Before you reach that stage, though, it is worthwhile considering which area immediately strikes you as something to which you feel you could dedicate the next 40 years of your working life.

However, it is highly advisable to start your career in general practice, working with household animals or even with larger animals on a farm, before you specialise in one of the more diverse forms of veterinary surgery.

Small-animal vet

The last RCVS survey in 2010 revealed that 69.4% of a vet's time is spent with small animals. The most common type of vet, a small-animal vet, works in local practice and deals with the care and treatment of household pets. You will be concerned with anything from vaccinations to neutering, as well as local surgery and general health check-ups. In unfortunate situations, you may be required to make the decision as to the kindness of putting an animal down to ease its pain.

Large-animal vet

Principally concerned with multiple animals in a group as opposed to individual animals, a large-animal vet is most often found on a farm, and is concerned with the health and productivity of the herd. Your responsibilities are likely to involve the treatment of disease and giving advice on the husbandry of the animals, including nutritional balance and sanitation. This role requires a strong will and a thick skin when dealing with farmers, who are an entirely different clientele to the ordinary public. Once you have the respect and confidence of the farmer, your job will be far easier.

Equine vet

As the name suggests, equine vets specialise in the treatment of horses. Stable and horse owners alike prefer to use a specialist equine vet when it comes to the treatment of their animals because horses are different from other animals in all respects – from anatomy to pharmacology. Horses also require different husbandry and therefore as a specialist you will be giving a different form of advice. Before specialising in this area, it is essential, or at least highly advisable, that you train in general practice as a smaller-animal vet and then progress to achieving your specialist qualifications later on once you have general experience to your name.

Exotic-animal vet

Exotic-animal vets have specialist training in the treatment of exotic animals including snakes and turtles. The term 'exotic' is wide-ranging, and it is worth remembering that ferrets and small rodents are included in this category. As with an equine vet, becoming a general vet first is a prerequisite before taking your specialist qualifications. There is an element of glamour in this work and you can expect to find yourself spending a lot of time at a zoo working with wild animals.

Avian vet

Avian vets are concerned with the treatment of birds, and this specialisation offers you a varied working environment. One day might be spent
in private practice, the next in a bird sanctuary and the next in a zoo. You
would certainly never be bored! The same advice applies as above: you
should take prior work in general practice before specialising with the
requisite qualifications, as working with smaller animals will help you
appreciate the smaller anatomical size of a bird.

Other types of vet

The vets listed above are the most common types of veterinary surgeons in the UK. However, this list is by no means comprehensive and,
should you wish to, you can also specialise in the following areas:

- cardiology (work based on the study of an animal's heart)
- dental (mouth-based work, including teeth, gums and hygiene)
- feline (working with cats, large and small, including zoo-based work)
- holistic (emphasises the study of all aspects of an animal's health,
  including physical, psychological, social, economic and cultural
  factors)
- marine (caring for marine-based animals such as dolphins and
  whales – strong swimming ability is a prerequisite).

The veterinary practice

There are many different types of veterinary practice. The majority, however, deal with all species. Others tend to specify the size of the animal,
i.e. some deal solely with larger animals, some smaller, and others only
equine. The size of practices varies a great deal. The average size is
three or four vets working together, but a few are smaller or much
larger. Some are incredibly busy, while others may manage to convey an
easier atmosphere while being equally hard-working. Some practices
offer particular facilities which define them as different types of veterinary practice.

The structure of a general practice

In a general practice, a veterinary surgeon is responsible for all types of
treatment, from medical to surgical, of all animals. It is not uncommon for
veterinary surgeons to study for further qualifications offered by the
RCVS while working in order to further their knowledge about certain
animals. Veterinary surgeons are vital to the practice and most start as a
locum or an associate. Most practices are partnerships run by several

veterinary surgeons with one principal. The goal of most associates working in a practice is to reach partnership level. This then involves separate
business skills in order to ensure that the practice is making money.

The principal, or practice manager, is usually found in a larger practice as
it is important to have one person who has a general overview of the
business. This person will be responsible for ensuring that all monies are
paid and that the practice is run to a high standard. This role is not common to all practices, as many cannot afford an extra level of support.

From a veterinary surgeon's point of view, the most important people
within the practice are veterinary nurses. They ensure that standards of
care are high and that both animals and owners are kept comfortable.
They assist in supportive care, and also undertake minor surgical procedures and tests, should they be required, and give the results to the
veterinary surgeons for treatment.

The receptionists are the first point of contact within a practice. A lot of
owners will be very disturbed when bringing their animal to the vet and
therefore it is the receptionist's responsibility to present a calm and
professional approach that will reassure the clients. They are also gate-
keepers and personal assistants for the veterinary surgeons, making
sure that appointments are managed and schedules are adhered to.

Veterinary practice as a small business

The veterinary practice is dependent upon the income it makes,
which is generated by the surgery itself, in order to be a successful
small business.

It does not receive money from an external source such as the government. The money that the practice makes is used to pay the staff and
the rent (if the site is not owned by the practice) and then the rest is put
back into the business to pay for equipment and up-to-date technology.

Vets are often faced with a moral dilemma when seeing a client who
cannot afford to pay the veterinary fees for their services. Fees can
often be very high and many clients (who are used to human healthcare
often being free of charge) are shocked by what they are required to
pay for the treatment of their pets. Vets need to be understanding in
this sort of situation but it's important to remember that you are part of
a business and this is your livelihood.

Accreditation

All practices need to adhere to the codes of practice of a specific
regulatory body.

RCVS accredited practice

The RCVS Practice Standards Scheme was launched on 1 January 2005. It is the only scheme representing the veterinary profession and is a regulatory body set up to ensure the highest standards. If you were to work in an RCVS-accredited practice, you would be dedicated to maintaining the highest possible standard of veterinary care; to providing a greater amount of information regarding the care of animals to the public and to clients; and to being at the cutting edge of advancements within the field of veterinary science.

BEVA listed practice

The British Equine Veterinary Association (BEVA) has compiled a list of self-certified practices in the equine industry and has a code of practice for veterinary surgeons in this field.

AVMA accredited course

The American Veterinary Medical Association is the North American accrediting council for veterinary surgeons. However, in order to practise medicine in North America, students must pass the North American Veterinary Licensing Examination (NAVLE).

EAEVE

The European Association of Establishments for Veterinary Education (EAEVE) provides assurance of the veterinary degree in Europe and its standards. The RVC, Copenhagen, Helsinki and Zurich/Bern are the only establishments that currently hold full accreditation.

Government service

In the public sector, veterinary surgeons are involved in protecting public health, working in government departments and agencies such as the Animal Health and Veterinary Laboratories Agency (AHVLA), the Food Standards Agency and the Veterinary Medicines Directorate. Defra employs vets to monitor animal health and to prevent the spread of diseases.

Most of the veterinary surgeons employed by Defra work in the Animal Health and Veterinary Laboratories Agency. Field officers have a wide range of responsibilities which include the control of major epidemic diseases of farm animals, matters of consumer protection (largely in relation to meat hygiene), the control of import and export of animals and the operation of health schemes.

The Animal Health and Veterinary Laboratories Agency comprises officers who are based in laboratories. Their job is to operate and support control schemes in the interests of public health, to monitor developments and give early warning of any disease problems or dangers to the safety of the food chain. They also provide practising vets with a chargeable diagnostic service. The Veterinary Laboratories Agency (VLA), which has now merged with the AHVLA at Weybridge, employs veterinary surgeons who carry out research and provide support for various field activities. The Veterinary Medicines Directorate deals with the licensing of drugs.

Veterinary teaching and research

Veterinary researchers play a vital role in advancing our understanding of diseases. Research in this field enhances the health, welfare and usefulness of both food-producing and companion animals, and helps to safeguard the public from diseases. Investigations of a comparative nature also help us to understand and manage human disease, for example in cancer, genetics, reproduction and infections. The majority of research takes place at the university veterinary schools and at research institutes (which, unlike veterinary practices, are financed by the government), in laboratories and in private enterprise. Many careers in research span the interface between human and veterinary medicine, which provides a huge scope for variety in the role.

A qualification in veterinary science is more than a licence to practise. It can also open up opportunities for those interested in university teaching and research at home and overseas. In addition to clinical research work, some veterinary surgeons undergo further postgraduate training in the biological sciences. Specialisation is possible in physiology, pathology, microbiology, nutrition, genetics and statistics. Veterinary scientists are not exclusively found working in institutions concerned with animal health and disease; they can also work in natural science laboratories, medical schools and medical research institutes. The opportunities are there for young veterinary surgeons attracted by a research career.

The veterinary schools are among those that provide referral hospitals to which veterinary surgeons can refer cases needing more specialised treatment. For example, recent success in the treatment of equine colic stemmed from early recognition and referral of appropriate cases allied to developments in anaesthesia and monitoring, improved surgical techniques and suture materials, plus better post-operative care. Good teamwork between the referring practitioner and the university specialists plays a big part.

Veterinary graduates are employed as research scientists by Defra, the Biotechnology and Biological Sciences Research Council, the Animal Health Trust, and in pharmaceutical and other industrial research organisations.

New trends

Membership of the EU has brought a new source of income into general practice. This comes about through increased certification required in the interests of safeguarding public health. Every abattoir has to have an official veterinary surgeon to see that it operates hygienically and that slaughtering is humane. Full-time vets are appointed to the Food Standards Agency to ensure that ethical practice is upheld in the slaughter of animals and hygiene and food safety for the general public. Every port and airport has to have a veterinary surgeon available.

Other career paths

The Army employs veterinary scientists in the Royal Army Veterinary Corps, where they care for service animals, mostly working dogs and horses used for ceremonial purposes. They also have public health responsibilities and opportunities for research or postgraduate study. Those recruited join with the rank of an Army captain for a four-year Short Service Commission, but this may be altered to a Regular Commission on application.

Some veterinary surgeons prefer to work for animal welfare societies, such as the RSPCA, PDSA and Blue Cross. Others work as inspectors for the Home Office.

Table 6 Number and distribution of members of the profession who are economically active in the UK only

Place of work	2011	2010	2009
General practice	15,371	14,843	14,269
Universities	956	889	811
Research councils	21	24	24
Industry and commerce	208	255	221
Charities	446	479	438
Government	815	844	804
Total	**17,817**	**17,334**	**16,567**

Table 7 Expected annual earnings

Salary	Region
£31,000	Wales
£29,400	Midlands
£34,000	South East
£54,643	London
£36,150	Yorkshire and North East
£53,000	East of England
£38,500	South West
£38,750	Scotland

Reprinted with kind permission from www.mysalary.co.uk

Veterinary nurses

Veterinary nurses work alongside veterinary surgeons and provide full support in veterinary surgeries or hospitals, ensuring the highest standard of care for the animals. Their work covers a wide range of duties, such as diagnostics (tests), treatments and minor surgery; they also are involved in major surgery, monitoring the animals while under anaesthetic. One crucial role of a veterinary nurse is education – teaching owners about animal husbandry. Veterinary nurses have good opportunities for career advancement and the longer they have worked in a particular practice, the more responsibility they will be given, for example managerial tasks such as managing teams either in a surgery or in an animal hospital. They will also be required to train new members of staff.

There are opportunities available in different environments too, such as veterinary research, universities, kennels and zoos. This can be an alternative career path for anyone who has not been able to obtain a place within a practice. The important thing to note is that there are lots of options.

In order to become a veterinary nurse, you need to train. This can either be on a vocational route or through higher education. They both allow you to register as a veterinary nurse. The vocational course is for those who prefer practical work. This Level 3 diploma can be obtained on either a full-time or a part-time basis while you work within a veterinary practice. The degree course is longer and more academic but it will open up opportunities in research in the future and in other careers, such as teaching. The latter course should be applied for via UCAS.

Women in the profession

Over three times as many women are now admitted to veterinary science courses as men. The table below forms part of a student survey published by the BVA. The figures might be rough approximations this year, but in most years the split is considered to be 80% female applicants to 20% male applicants. Therefore, gents, there is a balance to be addressed here!

Table 8 Number of male and female applicants

	All applicants	Degree accepts	Clearing accepts
Men	518	225	31
Women	1,734	746	115
Total	**2,252**	**971**	**146**

Women comprise about a third of all the vets in the country, but only one in five of the sole principals in general practice are women. Two explanations have been suggested for this. One is that the statistic reflects past intakes into the profession and this is changing. Another is that, whereas women are in the majority at age 26–35, they comprise only one in five of those aged 50 or over. This suggests that they leave the profession early – perhaps in order to have a family – and do not always return. The figures also hint that women are slightly more inclined than their male colleagues to work in the public sector.

Dealing with people

Being in veterinary practice means that you are running a business. This means that, for example, today's vets have to be familiar with computer records on health and know how to interpret them, but there is a more important factor: vets have to be customer-oriented. Students soon pick this up. 'The way we approach people is crucial; it's our bread and butter,' remarked one vet. 'It's the same on the telephone. We make a point of being cheerful and reassuring with a few words of advice until we can get there.' This aspect of practice is now so important that some practices hire a manager to run the administrative side and help to train reception staff. Most courses now make some attempt to introduce the student to the economics of running a practice, although, as one vet commented wryly: 'Few will think of bookkeeping!'

The professional approach

With increasing professionalism and rising customer expectations come higher overheads. While training, it is vital that a student realises the importance of everything that makes up a surgery. The establishment and maintenance of a modern veterinary surgery now require a considerable capital sum of money, so most newly qualified vets will start their career by going into practice with other vets. The most ambitious vet will aspire to and attain a partnership after two or three surgery moves; a few, after gaining experience over three or four years, will branch out on their own. Appreciating this is imperative for a vet because it helps you to map out your own career path: if you can understand what is required when working in practice, you can see what is essential and integral and this will help to shape your approach to your career and perhaps to a future surgery.

Summing up

Many students are interested in becoming veterinary surgeons. For some it will remain a pipe dream either because they lack the ability or skill, or because their ideas about being a veterinary surgeon are not rooted in reality. However, there are real opportunities for those who are motivated and determined to reach their goal. The competition is intense but not impossible and prospective students should be encouraged to explore the veterinary option early by seeking practical experience. As one vet put it: 'See a farm, get your wellies dirty, experience some blood and gore, and see that the life of a vet is not all about cuddly puppies!' This will test both resolve and suitability.

The demand for veterinary services and research-related activities is strong and is increasing. Market forces do dictate the number of places in veterinary schools, but funding limitations imposed by the higher education funding councils are also a controlling factor. Nevertheless, the profession of veterinary surgeon retains its popularity among young people. It is not because of the money, the car, or accommodation – which is often next to the practice ready for instant call-outs. Nor can the hours be the attraction; the provision of a 24-hour service to the public is mandatory. Rather, it is probably the sense that being a vet is a way of life rather than a job.

The unique skills a vet requires

An experienced vet, operating a mixed practice on the Wirral, put the unique qualities of being a vet this way: 'I think people respect what we do. Every Friday a lady brings us a chocolate cake. It's little things like this that make you feel appreciated.' A vet is many things – skilled surgeon, business manager, counsellor and confidant. Vets know that their animals are often the most important thing in their clients' lives. They have tremendous responsibility for the animals, whether in sickness or in health, and when all other options have failed they have the authority and power vested in them by law to take the animal's life. They devote their lives to animal welfare but their role is not based on sentimentality. Find out whether it is the life for you, and, if it is, go for it.

12| Don't count your chickens before they've hatched
Further information

Do not ever make the mistake of believing that you know enough, because you can always find out more. If you want to be the cat that got the cream, do your research. You will be more likely to get to your number one choice of university if you do your own investigations about where you want to go.

Remember, there is no harm in entering into a dialogue with an admissions tutor if you are asking pertinent and considered questions. An elephant never forgets and neither does an admissions tutor.

Listed below are the contact details of the veterinary schools in the UK and websites of other organisations that might help your research.

Veterinary schools in the UK

Bristol
Department of Clinical Veterinary Science
University of Bristol
Langford House
Langford BS40 5DU
Tel (veterinary admissions): 0117 928 9280
Fax (general admissions): 0117 928 9505
Email: vet-ug-admissions@bristol.ac.uk
Website: www.bris.ac.uk

Cambridge
Veterinary Admission Enquiries Adviser
Department of Veterinary Medicine
University of Cambridge
Madingley Road
Cambridge CB3 0ES
Tel: 01223 330811
Fax: 01223 337610
Email: application.advice@vet.cam.ac.uk
Website: www.vet.cam.ac.uk

Edinburgh

The Admissions Officer
Royal (Dick) School of Veterinary Studies
University of Edinburgh
Easter Bush Campus
Midlothian EH25 9RG
Tel: 0131 651 7305
Fax: 0131 650 6585
Email: vetug@ed.ac.uk
Website: www.ed.ac.uk/schools-departments/vet

Glasgow

Admissions Office
School of Veterinary Medicine
University of Glasgow
Bearsden Road
Glasgow G61 1QH
Tel: 0141 330 2225
Fax: 0141 942 7215
Email: vet-sch-admissions@glasgow.ac.uk
Website: www.gla.ac.uk/schools/vet

Liverpool

Admissions Sub-Dean
School of Veterinary Science
Thompson Yates Building
University of Liverpool
Liverpool L69 3GB
Tel: 0151 794 4797
Email: vetadmit@liverpool.ac.uk
Website: www.liv.ac.uk/veterinary-science/

London

The Registry
Royal Veterinary College
University of London
Royal College Street
London NW1 0TU
Tel: 020 7468 5147
Fax: 020 7468 5311
Email: enquiries@rvc.ac.uk
Website: www.rvc.ac.uk

Nottingham

Admissions Team
School of Veterinary Medicine and Science
University of Nottingham
Sutton Bonington Campus
College Road

Sutton Bonington LE12 5RD
Tel: 0115 951 6464
Fax: 0115 951 6415
Email: veterinary-enquiries@nottingham.ac.uk
Website: www.nottingham.ac.uk/vet

Other contacts and sources of information

Useful organisations and websites

- Animal Welfare Foundation: www.bva-awf.org.uk
- Blue Cross: www.bluecross.org.uk
- British Equine Veterinary Association: www.beva.org.uk
- British Veterinary Association (this is the national representative body for the British veterinary profession): www.bva.co.uk
- Department for Environment, Food and Rural Affairs (Defra): www.defra.gov.uk
- Mander Portman Woodward: www.mpw.co.uk
- People's Dispensary for Sick Animals: www.pdsa.org.uk

Royal College of Veterinary Surgeons
Belgravia House
62–64 Horseferry Road
London SW1P 2AF
Tel: 020 7222 2001
Email: education@rcvs.org.uk
Website: www.rcvs.org.uk

St George's University
University Centre
Grenada
West Indies
Tel: 0800 169 9061
Email: SGUEnrolment@sgu.edu
Website: www.sgu.edu

University of Medicine in Kosice, Slovak Republic
Recruitment (XLNC)
Application to Faculty of Medicine
UPJS in Kosice
Matuskova 18
04011 Kosice
Slovak Republic
Email: info@medicinekosice.eu
Website: www.medicinekosice.eu

Society of Practising Veterinary Surgeons
www.spvs.org.uk
Provides advice to veterinary surgeons.

Super Vets
www.rvc.ac.uk/supervets
Website for the BBC series about vets at the Royal Veterinary College, London Zoo and Whipsnade Wild Animal Park.

Universities and Colleges Admissions Service
www.ucas.com

Vetsonline
www.vetsonline.com
Online database and resource.

GOV.UK
www.gov.uk/student-finance
Information on student loans and grants.

Courses

VetCam
Tel: 01223 330811
Two-day residential 'Introduction to Veterinary Science in Cambridge' course, held in March.

Vetsim
www.workshop-uk.net/vetsim
Conference organised by Workshop Conferences for interested sixth-formers and held annually in Nottingham.

Publications

Getting into Oxford & Cambridge: 2014 entry (publication date April 2013), Jenny Blaiklock,Trotman, £12.99.

Cut the Cost of Uni: How to graduate with less debt, Gwenda Thomas, Trotman, £9.99.

HEAP 2014: University Degree Course Offers, 44th edition (publication date May 2013), Brian Heap, Trotman, £35.

How to Complete Your UCAS Application: 2014 Entry, 25th edition (publication date May 2013), Beryl Dixon, Trotman, £12.99.
Works through the application procedure step by step using examples, and includes information on how to avoid the most common mistakes and how to write a winning personal statement.

Student loans – a guide to terms and conditions 2012/13
Free from the Student Loans Company, 100 Bothwell Street, Glasgow G2 7JD or www.slc.co.uk.

Glossary

Admissions tutor
The person in charge of your application.

American Veterinary Medical Association (AVMA)
The AVMA represents US veterinarians, providing information, publications and resources such as training courses.

Animal Health and Veterinary Laboratories Agency (AHVLA)
Working on behalf of Defra throughout Great Britain, the AHVLA was established to ensure animal health and welfare and public health.

Animal husbandry
An agricultural term meaning breeding and raising livestock.

Bachelor of Veterinary Medicine (BVetMed)
A bachelor's degree for studies in the United Kingdom. Most courses are five years in length, although Cambridge has a six-year course and chooses to award a Bachelor of Arts (BA) after three years, followed by a Bachelor of Veterinary Medicine (VetMB) after six years.

BioMedical Admissions Test (BMAT)
This examination is taken by students looking to apply for veterinary medicine at the Royal Veterinary College and University of Cambridge. The University of Bristol has access to the results for research purposes only; they do not form part of the offer.

Bovine spongiform encephalopathy (BSE)
Commonly referred to as mad cow disease, BSE is a neurological disease that affects the brains of cattle. The human form of the disease is Creutzfeldt–Jakob disease (CJD).

Bovine tuberculosis (bTB)
Bovine tuberculosis is a serious disease in cattle. It is said to be commonly spread by badgers, which are a protected species, and therefore the debate remains over whether badgers should be culled.

British Equine Veterinary Association (BEVA)
The BEVA is the leading body for the equine veterinary profession. It ensures high standards throughout the profession, has 2,400 members globally and also runs outstanding continuing professional development (CPD) courses.

Clinical years
The third and fourth years of veterinary medicine.

Continuing professional development (CPD)
The Royal College of Veterinary Surgeons' Code of Professional Conduct for Veterinary Surgeons states that veterinary surgeons have a responsibility to 'maintain and develop the knowledge and skills relevant to their professional practice and competence'. A minimum amount of 105 hours over an ongoing three-year period is recommended for CPD, with an average of 35 hours per year.

Department for Environment, Food and Rural Affairs (Defra)
The government department that looks after environmental protection, agriculture, food production standards, fisheries and rural communities in the United Kingdom. It is responsible for maintaining high standards within the industries.

European Association of Establishments for Veterinary Education (EAEVE)
The EAEVE aims to harmonise the standards of veterinary tuition in the European Union, giving confidence to members of the public and veterinary professionals.

Extramural rotations (EMR)
EMR are undertaken by students studying at veterinary school and the time is divided between farming work and experience in veterinary practice.

Extramural studies (EMS)
EMS are studies that take place outside the university setting. The Royal College of Veterinary Surgeons states that students must complete 38 weeks of EMS during their course: 12 weeks of pre-clinical and 26 weeks of clinical placements.

Foot-and-mouth disease (FMD)
FMD is a viral disease that affects cattle, pigs, sheep, goats and deer. Hedgehogs and rats can also become infected, and people, cats, dogs and game animals can carry infected material. FMD is more contagious than any other animal disease, and the mortality rate among young animals is high.

Fresher
A first-year undergraduate student.

Integrated course
A course that teaches lots of different disciplines which all come together in the final year of study. The individual elements are taught by specialists in disciplines ranging from pharmacology to anatomy.

International English Language Testing System (IELTS)

An English test used to determine the level of language ability for international students. A typical score of 7.0 is required.

Intramural rotations (IMR)

IMR take place in the clinical years of veterinary medicine, and are designed to develop and utilise skills you have previously learnt. You will work in clinical teams and have access to clinical records. This will encourage you to present a professional image.

Master of Science (MSc)

The MSc is typically a taught programme over one or two years, depending on the university.

Methicillin-resistant *Staphylococcus aureus* (MRSA)

MRSA, commonly known as the 'superbug', is a human-based infection found in hospitals but it can also colonise and cause infections in pets and farm animals.

Multiple choice questions (MCQs)

MCQs are used in some veterinary examinations.

National Scholarship Programme (NSP)

Students resident in England whose family income is less than £25,000 per year are eligible for a grant to help with tuition fees, accommodation or living costs from the NSP.

North American Veterinary Licensing Examination (NAVLE)

In order to practise in North America, students must pass the NAVLE.

People's Dispensary for Sick Animals (PDSA)

The PDSA is a veterinary charity that offers healthcare for a range of animals.

Pharmacodynamics

The study of the mechanism of the action of drugs and how they affect the body.

Pharmacokinetics

The study of the absorption, distribution, metabolism and excretion of drugs.

Pre-clinical years

The first two years of veterinary medicine.

Professional Development Phase (PDP)

The first year after completing your degree is the PDP, when you are expected to develop your skills.

Royal College of Veterinary Surgeons (RCVS)

The regulatory body for all veterinary professionals in the United Kingdom. The RCVS's role is to ensure the health and welfare of animals and the efficient practice of veterinary professionals and to provide an impartial opinion on animal health and disease as well as on the latest debates.

Royal Society for the Prevention of Cruelty to Animals (RSPCA)
The leading UK charity specialising in the care, control and rescue of animals.

Royal Veterinary College (RVC)
The oldest and largest of the veterinary schools in the United Kingdom and one of the world's leading specialist veterinary schools.

Test of English as a Foreign Language (TOEFL)
An English test used to determine the level of language ability for international students. A score of 93 or higher is required.

Therapeutics
The use of drugs in the prevention and treatment of disease.

University College Admissions System (UCAS)
The central body through which students apply to veterinary schools; you do not apply to the universities directly. You can choose four veterinary courses and one non-veterinary course.

Veterinary Laboratories Agency (VLA)
Centre set up to operate and support control schemes in the interests of public health, to monitor developments and give early warning of any disease problems or dangers to the safety of the food chain. Now part of the Animal Health and Veterinary Laboratories Agency.

Veterinary Medicines Directorate (VMD)
The VMD deals with the licensing of drugs.